Beyond _{The}Shadows

Embracing Authentic Worship

Beyond
The Shadows

Embracing Authentic Worship

T. C. Smith

SMYTH&HELWYS
PUBLISHING, INCORPORATED • MACON, GEORGIA

Smyth & Helwys Publishing, Inc.
6316 Peake Road
Macon, Georgia 31210-3960
1-800-747-3016
©2000 by Smyth & Helwys Publishing
All rights reserved.
Printed in the United States of America.

T. C. Smith

The paper used in this publication meets the minimum
requirements of American National Standard for Information
Sciences—Permanence of Paper for Printed Library Materials.
ANSI Z39.48–1984. (alk. paper)

All biblical quotations are taken from the New Revised
Standard Version (NRSV) unless otherwise indicated.

Library of Congress Cataloging-in-Publication Data

Smith, T. C. (Taylor Clarence), 1915–
    Beyond the shadows: embracing authentic worship.
    pp.   cm.
    Includes bibliographical references.
    (alk. paper)
    1. God—Worship and love.
    2. Christian life—Baptist authors.
    I. Title.
    BV4817.S55   2000
    248.3—dc21   99-39703
                                                CIP

    ISBN 1-57312-267-X

Contents

Preface

I became a Christian at the age of nine and was baptized into Christ at First Baptist Church in Pineville, Louisiana, the first of seventeen Baptist churches where I have held membership during my eighty-five years. Many changes have taken place in my pilgrimage since that time. At times I have experienced shadows that have separated me from true worship of God.

I began teaching Sunday School at the age of seventeen and have taught New Testament studies at five theological seminaries or divinity schools and at two universities. I have served as pastor of a Baptist congregation and as interim pastor of seven Baptist churches. For thirty years I was a chaplain in the Naval Reserve Chaplain Corps. My preaching engagements number more than a hundred different churches. Included in this list are not only Baptist churches, but also other Protestant communions, military chapels, two Roman Catholic churches, and a Jewish synagogue. What is written in this book comes from experiences and observations of my own manner of worship and from that of other faith traditions.

My purpose in writing this book is not to severely criticize the manner in which people worship God, but rather to show distractions that lead us away from the center of the Christian faith. My purpose is also to create an atmosphere of debate and thought-provoking reflection.

There are those who say that we live in a post-Christian world where Christianity no longer plays a role in shaping social and cultural life and its beliefs no longer have the public presence they once had. To counter this claim, some would appeal to statistics that guarantee most people believe in God. Others might allude to the large attendance in churches, synagogues, and mosques or to the vast amounts of money given to these institutions. Yet people can honor God with their lips when their hearts are far away.

Some persons believe that if we think critically, it is a sign of unbelief. God gave us the endowment to think critically. How can we be sure of what is true or false, good or bad, right or wrong unless we can make judgments? If we depend on the authority of a subjective experience and cannot think critically and rationally so as to base our conclusions on objective facts, our religion becomes a sort of grab-bag affair. The goal of the Christian witness is not success, nor are the means for attaining that goal a particular method or technique. Rather, it is the proclamation of the truth of Christianity as it unfolds in the New Testament.

The chapters in this book are based on lectures and discussions I presented at Furman University Learning in Retirement (FULIR). The members of the class were very helpful in relating their own shadows in the worship of God and in sharing observations of others. I am indebted to the class members for their encouragement to continue this writing project.

I am also indebted to my wife, Ellen Bernice, who aided me in smoothing out some of the obscure portions when she proofread the manuscript.

Introduction

In 1998 the Barna Research Group polled a cross-section of American Christians concerning their opinions of worship. When asked what worship meant, two out of three said they did not know, or they offered responses such as "attend church," "being a church," or "believing God exists." Only a fourth said that worship is for the sake of honoring God. Some believed worship is all about a busy round of activities.

The researchers also discovered that some persons evaluate worship on the basis of a large attendance and great enthusiasm. To others, the purpose of worship is to please people. They especially noted the desire for performance-oriented music and entertaining preaching. The report cited that the first criterion of worship should be how many people experience God. Worship experience is more important in Christian development than just a large attendance in the church.

True religion has always been in conflict with false religion. The religion of reality has always been in opposition to a religion that relies on profession and outward form. What is true of religion in general is equally true for Judeo-Christian faith in particular. Jews and Christians of the past and present continue to worship God in the shadows.

There are many definitions of the word "shadow." Throughout this book, shadow is defined as "something without reality or substance" or "protection" or "shelter."

The word "worship" comes from the Old English word *weorthscipe*, which means "worth-ship." Therefore, when we worship, we declare the great worth of God, who is the ultimate in life. In the Old Testament the general word for worship is the Hebrew word *abodah*, which comes from the verb *abad*, meaning "to labor or to serve," and the substantive is usually translated "the service of God." To describe a specific act of worship, the word *hishtahawah* is frequently used. Its root is in the verb *shaha*, meaning "to bow or prostrate oneself." The New Testament Greek word *latreia* corresponds to the word *abodah*, and *hishtahawah* is replaced by *proskunein*, meaning "to prostrate oneself, adore and worship."

In our Judeo-Christian tradition, worship is both external and internal. It is involved with our service to God in obedience to God's will, but it is also a spiritual attitude. Both of these have their place in private and public worship.

When we declare the worth of God internally, we express toward God reverence, adoration, homage, gratitude, confession, praise, and honor. But this sentiment should not remain on the level of mere recognition. People must be moved by this experience to participate in the intention of God by pursuing truth, goodness, mercy, love, and peace. Obedience to God's will should follow the feeling of awe and reverence for God.

In Luke10:25-28 a lawyer put Jesus to the test by asking the question, "Teacher, what must I do to inherit eternal life?" Jesus replied, "What is written in the law? What do you read there?" Then the lawyer answered with a combination of Deuteronomy 6:5 and Leviticus 19:18, "You shall love the Lord your God with all your heart, and with all your soul, and with all your strength, and with all your mind; and your neighbor as yourself." After the lawyer said this, Jesus commended him for giving the right answer and went on to say,

"Do this, and you will live." Jesus was showing the lawyer that there is a great hiatus between profession and practice, between proclamation and performance. It is possible for us to recognize a truth without intending to put the truth into practice. In worship we proclaim the worth of God, but of what value is the declaration unless we translate into everyday life those qualities of God that are recognized as being of supreme value?

After the Israelites settled in the land of Canaan, they began to shelter themselves with shadows in the worship of Yahweh who had led them out of Egypt, given them commandments, and brought them into the land promised to Abraham. They took refuge in the ark of covenant, the tabernacle and later the Temple, and a religion of the altar with its elaborate sacrifices. Many did not trust Yahweh to bring rain and fertility to the soil so that they could have an abundant crop. Thus they began to worship the Baalim, the gods of fertility and agriculture of the Canaanites. To produce and achieve, the Israelites believed they must follow the gods of the land.

In the history of the faith of Israel, the prophets constantly called the people back to sincere faith and at the same time denounced their sham beliefs. Amos, a son of the Southern Kingdom, went to Bethel in the Northern Kingdom. In his denunciation of the cultic practice he said,

> I hate, I despise your festivals, and I take no delight in your solemn assemblies. Even though you offer me your burnt offerings and grain offerings, I will not accept them; and the offerings of well-being of your fatted animals I will not look upon. Take away from me the noise of your songs; I will not listen to the melody of your harps. But let justice roll down like waters, and righteousness like an everflowing stream. (Amos 5:21-24)

The prophet Hosea's ministry followed closely upon that of Amos in the Northern Kingdom. He was a native of the north, whereas Amos was from the south. Like Amos, Hosea scathed his countrymen and said in behalf of Yahweh, "For I desire steadfast love and not sacrifice, the knowledge of God rather than burnt offerings" (Hos 6:6).

In the same denunciatory vein as Amos and Hosea, Micah, the prophet from the Southern Kingdom, proclaimed doom upon the people. He saw them worshiping God in the shadows of the sacrifices and rituals. In his oracles he proclaimed:

> With what shall I come before the Lord, and bow myself before God on high? Shall I come before him with burnt offerings, with calves a year old? Will the Lord be pleased with thousands of rams, with ten thousands of rivers of oil? Shall I give my firstborn for my transgression, the fruit of my body for the sin of my soul?" He has told you, O mortal, what is good; and what does the Lord require of you but to do justice, and to love kindness, and to walk humbly with your God? (Mic 6:6-8)

The historical Isaiah, a contemporary of Micah, Amos, and Hosea, followed in the prophetic tradition and attacked the social injustice in the land of Judah. The people of Judah were saying to him, "This is a great day for Yahweh worship." They directed his attention toward the court of the Temple, filled with worshipers offering multitudes of sacrifices. But Isaiah was not fooled. He saw a form of religion, but the people had nothing to do with it as a force. He criticized their burnt offerings, incense, new moon and sabbath observances, and solemn assemblies. Isaiah cried out, "Hear, O heavens, and listen O earth . . . The ox knows its owner, and the donkey its master's crib; but Israel does not know, my people do not understand" (Isa 1:2-3). Isaiah continued by telling the people that their hands were filled with the blood of injustice and oppression.

About a century later, Jeremiah, facing the threat of an imminent invasion of Judah by the Babylonians, denounced fiercely the people of Judah because they committed two evils. They forsook the fountain of living waters and constructed cisterns that contained stagnant water at the bottom of a leaky cistern. Judah had forsaken their God-given freedom and had become a slave to Assyria and Egypt. Later the people put their trust in the Temple in Jerusalem. They yelled, "the temple of the Lord, the temple of the Lord," thinking God would not allow the city to be taken because God resided in the Temple. Jeremiah did not take any stock in such a shadow of worship, however.

These and other prophets condemned the populist religion. They condemned the shrines at Bethel, Gilgal, and Beersheba among others. They censured the worship in the national temple at Jerusalem, which was a rallying place for loyalty to kings and the cultic worship of Yahweh. They also spoke against the Baalim.

It is quite possible that Judaism would have disappeared from history along with the religion of the Philistines, Ammonites, Moabites, Hittites, and others groups had it not been for the prophets. Judaism might have been nothing more than an ephemeral tribal cult swept away in the dust bin of history. The prophets preserved the essentials in the religion of Israel and kept the people from worshiping God in the shadows. It was not the trappings of a bloody altar, or a God-box ark of the covenant, or a smoking incense pot, or the Temple itself, or the cultic mumbo-jumbo of the priests that survived the ravages of time. Rather, it was the clear word of God from the prophets.

From the early part of the fourth century BC until the first century AD, the prophetic voice was not heard in Judaism. During that time, however, the Pharisees arose as the interpreters of revelation, claiming to be in the prophetic succession. But unlike the prophets, their authority was not based on having received a word from the prophets, but on the explanation of what the prophetic revelation and the Law conveyed.

When Jesus was on earth, he faced much opposition from the Pharisees. They believed in the supremacy of the Law. They had power to regulate the ritual in the Temple and perhaps would have ultimately abolished the Temple and used the synagogue as a substitute had the Temple not been destroyed by the Romans in AD 70. Along with the written law the Pharisees developed an oral tradition. This oral tradition in the New Testament is known by the tradition of the elders. It acted as a fence to keep the people from violating the written law. In time, the oral law came to have equal value in Judaism with the written law. Jesus criticized the tradition of the elders and at times even the written law. Actually, the Law became a roof to shield the Pharisees from true worship of God. They worshiped God in the shadows through a kind of worship of the Law.

The apostle Paul faced heresy that was brewing in Colossae and wrote a letter to the church to guide the congregation through the heresy. Paul had not evangelized the people in Colossae. This had been done by Epaphras, a fellow-worker of Paul. Somehow Paul got wind of the strange teachings and wrote this letter to lead the Colossians out of the darkness of mistaken notions. The teaching errors seemed to have stemmed from astral religion and a syncretism of Judaism, Christianity, and paganism. In this epistle the author sought to gather into the briefest compass those things that were essential for the Christian faith and at the same time expose the errors of the false teachers. It is impossible for us to know all the details about the heresy. There is still a mystery about the full nature of the false teachings, but for the recipients of the letter there was no mystery. They knew exactly to what Paul referred.

The pagan theories the Christians of Colossae adopted were mere guesswork and not founded on reality. In Colossians 2, Paul touches on features of heretical practices in Colossae, noting that these were mere shadows and not the substance of worship. He also speaks of the worship of angels. Apparently the people at Colossae recognized that God was absolute and so transcendent that one had to worship God through intermediaries in whom divine nature was partially reflected.

Perhaps we are all guilty at some point in our Christian pilgrimage of dabbling in the shadows, and it is extremely difficult at times to distinguish between the real or substance of the Christian faith. But to become mature Christians, it is incumbent upon us to shake ourselves loose from the protective shields that ward off God. In the chapters that follow, we shall confront some of the ways we worship God in the shadows.

Chapter 1

A Book Religion

In a feature article in the *Charlotte Observer* about thirty-six years ago, Harry Golden said, "The Bible gets more lip service than any other book in history. It has produced more titles and books than any other historical event." What Golden said in the 1960s is true now. There is no scarcity of Bibles in the world. The Bible has been translated into almost every language and dialect. We have more than our share of English versions—the Authorized Version, the New American Standard Version, the New Revised Standard Version, the New English Bible, Today's English Version, the Jerusalem Bible, and the New International Version. In addition, we have an abundance of individual translations—Goodspeed, Montgomery, Moffatt, Weymouth, Phillips, Williams, the Living Bible, and others.

Although the Bible enjoys the greatest number of all book sales, there is greater ignorance of its contents than of any other book's. It suffers more from praise than from intensive reading. Furthermore, there are those who use it in a superficial manner to promote their own causes. For example:

• The Bible is used in time of war to build up morale so that it can improve a person's capacity to kill.
• The parable of the talents is employed to support capitalism.

- The parable of the laborers in the vineyard is exploited to embrace a living wage, *laissez-faire* economics, a Protestant work ethic, and social security.
- The statement in Acts 2:44 that they "had all things in common" has been used to support communism.
- Segregationists take their stand on the Hamitic curse. (In reality, it was a curse on Ham's son Canaan who had done nothing wrong. It is quite clear from the Genesis account of this event that the curse was sent from Noah, not God. Furthermore, Noah was drunk when he pronounced the curse and did not know what he was saying.)
- Some people use Daniel and Revelation to proclaim the termination of the age and as a calendar by which God will deal with the world.
- Some political/religious activitists use *cherem* in the Old Testament as a basis for dropping nuclear bombs on our enemies.
- Jesus' name has been dishonored by those who thought they were following in his footsteps.
- The cause of Christ has been exploited to endorse slavery and other evils in society.
- Many times when we close our prayers in the name of Christ, God's character is dishonored because our prayers are not commensurate with the character of God revealed in Christ.
- A person guided by self-interest can take a verse or passage of Scripture out of context and make it mean whatever s/he wants it to mean.

If we have the open Bible and come to it with a closed mind, we can turn the words into darkness rather than light.

It is always easy to believe the Bible from cover to cover, even the genuine leather on the cover, without knowing its contents. This was true of the Zealots in the day of Jesus. They were willing to fight for the Law, but they had little knowledge of it. People can boast about the Bible being the bestselling book and that it is translated in most of the languages of the world, but if it is not read with the desire to know its meaning for life, it becomes useless.

Fundamentalists tremble with fear if they are forced to admit there are inconsistencies, differences, doublets, and contradictions in the Bible. To evade these problems, some Christians choose verses and quote them out of context. They emphatically state, "The Bible says," but they fail to ask important questions such as these: Where does it say this? In what situation and under what conditions was the statement made? If we are not careful, we may be guilty of confining God between the covers of a book.

Our faith is not dependent upon the credibility of the biblical writers; it is dependent upon the fullness of God's revelation in Jesus Christ. The yoke of inerrancy is one that our ancestors were unable to bear. Philo, a first-century Jewish philosopher of Alexandria, Egypt, believed that the Scriptures were written while the authors were in a state of ecstasy that obliterated human powers. He even stated that the holy oracles came by divine ventriloquism. Doubtless, Philo went beyond what a modern-day fundamentalist would say with respect to the manner in which Scripture has come to us. Yet, interestingly enough, it was Philo who first observed that there are two creation stories in Genesis. By the use of Platonic philosophy he declared that the man created in Genesis 1:27 was heavenly, while the man in Genesis 2:7 was earthly. Philo was also well aware of contradictions, inconsistencies, and doublets, but he was able to overcome these to his own satisfaction by allegorizing these under the influence of the Stoics.

For some Christians, the very thought of using a critical method in an approach to the Bible is taboo. Yet they do not object to making a critical inquiry into other types of literature. Why is a distinction made here? Is there a fear that such an inquiry will nullify faith? Is there an attempt to defend God? God needs no defense. If we as frail and unworthy human beings have to defend God, perhaps we are not worshiping the true God of the universe. There are uncritical lovers of the Bible, and there are unloving critics of the Bible. Both of these are in error. The most sensible approach is being a loving critic of the Bible.

Some people look upon the Bible as a book of science, especially when it comes to the Genesis creation account. They avidly oppose those who set forth a theory of evolution or of the "Big Bang." They counter by saying that the Genesis story is fact. How do these persons know? This story is also a theory, not a confirmed fact. The writer of Genesis 1 adopted a Babylonian myth, the *Enuma Elish*, to prove that the God of Israel, not the Babylonian god Marduk, created the universe. While some view the Bible from a scientific viewpoint, others scurry to the Bible as the ancients scampered to the oracle at Delphi or the witch of Endor and as people of our times rush to an astrologist to get a view of the future. The Bible thereby becomes a book of predictions, a crystal ball to gaze into the unknown.

Some view the Bible as a sort of good luck charm. It is something they can touch for good fortune. When I was eight years of age, my friends and I customarily played a game with the Bible. We were told that if we made a wish and at random opened the Bible three times, our wish would come true—provided that in the three tries we found the expression, "And it came to pass." Of course, that was when we had access only to the King James Version; other versions do not have this expression. For us, the Bible became a wish book.

We have stated what the Bible *is not*. Now let us consider what the Bible *is*. It is a record of the revelation of God to humanity through nature, by God's mighty acts in history, and in the consciousness of individuals. It is an account of God's action in revealing God's self and humankind's response, positive or negative, to that revelation. It is also a record of people's understanding of the revelation in accordance with their spiritual receptiveness. In this library of sixty-six books, extending in time for a thousand years and covering two continents, we become spectators and participants in the drama of human history. This book deals with the human situation. There are stories of rape, murder, incest, trickery, war, religious persecution, church fights, heavenly visions, hope, and faith.

The Bible was written in different languages and styles and in different ages. Its authors were shepherds, farmers, warriors, poets, priests, prophets, historians, kings, a converted Pharisee, Jewish Christians, apostles, and scribes. The Bible is not purely a human book, nor is it purely divine. The divine and the human are intertwined. By considering the human authors of the Bible as passive instruments under the complete control of God, and producing documents for which God is totally responsible, the Bible supposedly becomes uniform on all levels of revelation. However, a cursory reading of the Old Testament reveals to the average reader a great contrast between the revelation of God's character over against the New Testament presentation.

Some readers are offended by the Bible's primitive barbaric images of God, subhuman ethics, and perverse nationalism. Without listing the numerous discrepancies, doublets, and inaccurate statements in the Old Testament—that are inevitable as long as imperfect individuals write—there is a matter of more vital importance. This is the view of God's character presented in certain portions of the Old Testament. Did God command the Israelites to institute *cherem,* the absolute annihilation of their enemies and property with no exemptions—not even the old men, women, children, and babies? Over against this picture we have the final revelation of God in Jesus Christ who said, "Love your enemies and pray for those who persecute you" (Matt 5:44).

In the Old Testament the most shocking things are done in the name of God. Consider the number of psalms that invoke curses upon the enemies of Israel. Do these reflect the true character of God? There are certain psalms that my Christian conscience will not permit me to read in front of a congregation unless I delete certain objectionable verses.

What we know of God in the Old Testament is valid if it is consistent with the revelation of God in Christ. That which is not consistent with the revelation of God in Christ is not of God, but is a failure of Israel to comprehend clearly God's revealing activity. Does this mean that the Old Testament, which has an inferior revelation in some sections, is no longer of value to us? Should we discard the Old Testament as Marcion did in the second century? Not at all. Marcion was troubled because he saw a great contrast between the character of God presented in the Old Testament and the character of God revealed in Christ. In his day, biblical exegesis afforded him only one alternative to overcome this conflict— an allegorical interpretation of the Scriptures initiated by Philo. He refused to take that exit.

While the criterion by which we evaluate the Old Testament is the authority of Christ, it is essential for us to have the Old Testament so that we can understand the New Testament. Not only should we use the Old Testament for this purpose, but we should also use apocryphal writings, rabbinical literature, archaeology, and historical data. Rather than stressing the contrast between the revelation of God in the Bible, we should look for the continuity. God, who was revealed in the Old Testament, was revealed completely in Christ. In both Testaments it is the same revealing God. However, since humanity could not fully comprehend the character of God in nature, the events of history, and human consciousness, God came to us in the flesh in Jesus Christ.

God's revelation did not come through a book, but through persons. Thus the trustworthiness of God's revelation in the Old Testament is largely dependent upon the individual through whom this revelation came. We can hardly imagine that the author's selfhood was suspended when he was inspired to write about the revelation he received from God. His message was always related to his own thought and outlook, and the form he gave to it was his own casting. Therefore, as such, it was not a perfect word from God even if it had abiding significance. It is not that God progressively revealed God's self, as some suppose, but individuals progressively understood the givenness of God. This gradual understanding of God cannot be measured chronologically on an upward scale because in the history of Israel there were heights and depths of comprehension on the pilgrimage.

The Reformers did not consciously make of the Bible a paper pope to compete with the Roman Pontiff. They were involved in a controversy that was conducted under the rules of the scholastic system, the only scholarship known in their time. The scholastic system centered around definitions, formulation of theses, and appeals to the authority of church and tradition. To combat this system with the authority of the Bible, they resorted to proof texts from Scripture, seeing before them the need for a literal and verbal inerrency of the

Bible. Calvin constructed a complete system of theology and buttressed it with proof texts. In their witnessing, the Reformers insisted that the authority of the Scriptures was not in the letter but in the spirit. Yet when they formulated doctrines, their emphasis shifted to the literal meaning of the text and the proper intellectual understanding of its theological teaching.

The successors of the Reformers deserted the true Protestant position in two ways. First, they began to worship the letter of the Bible. They claimed the Bible was an infallible book. Because it was the verbally inspired revelation of God's truth, it must be perfect in every respect. The upshot of this kind of reasoning prompted the Swiss churches in 1675 to declare that no barbarism or solecism had ever entered the Greek text and that the vowel points of the Hebrew text were divinely inspired. Second, the infallibility of the Scriptures to which they appealed for authority was nothing more that an infallibility of a theological system based on the false idea of the infallibility of interpretation of the Scriptures.

There are advantages and disadvantages in having a written tradition, or a "book religion." Note the following lists:

Advantages
- less possibility of changes or corruptions
- can be translated into other languages
- availability for careful and continued study
- can be used as a criterion of religious truth

Disadvantages
- contemporary language, culture, and thought-forms must be used
- expressions may be labeled as archaic and irrelevant

- translations into other languages necessary, making possible mistranslation or misrepresentation
- subject to different cultures, customs, social structures, and political motivations
- can become bibliolatry (worship of the Bible)

The authority of God is manifested in three areas: the Bible, the community of believers, and the individual. All three of these are secondary authorities. They become authoritative only when they reflect the primary and supreme authority.

The troubling temptation of Christians is to search for a secondary authority to use as a shield to ward off an encounter with God. The Pharisees had scripture, yet their sacred literature was used as a shelter to escape the revelation of God in Christ. They took refuge in their own interpretations of the Law and built a fence around the intention of God with their oral tradition. The Jews thought they had the Law contained when the oral tradition was codified and the Mishnah came into being. Then they interpreted the Mishnah and compiled the Babylonian and Palestinian Talmuds, thinking they had God in a box.

If we depend solely on the information contained in the Bible, and our belief rests solely on this specified content, our religion becomes secondhand or a worship of the document. To become part of this community of believers in the pages of Scriptures, we must have a personal relationship with God to whom the message of the Bible points. Without this personal experience, all else becomes unintelligible chatter.

Millions of Christians will affirm that they accept the authority of the Bible in its totality, yet they may have never read enough of it to come to any conclusion of their own. Their judgment is based almost entirely on what others have told them. If they follow those who have shut God in a book and accept an impersonal authority of a sacred document rather than the personal authority of a living God, they begin to worship the witness material rather than the God to whom the material refers. The belief in infallible Scripture or an infallible church is an effort by Christians to make God's hidden sovereignty visible, tangible, and controllable to the extent that they displace the position that God alone occupies.

Chapter 2

Sacramental Words

In its original meaning given by the Romans, the Latin word *sacramentum* (sacrament) was an oath used especially for the military. When a soldier entered the Roman army, he gave an oath of allegiance to his commander. In his letter to the emperor Trajan in AD 112, Pliny said that he had found Christians in Asia Minor who bound themselves with an oath (*sacramentum*). We understand him to mean that the Christians had pledged allegiance to Christ. The technical ecclesiastical usage of sacrament has been attributed to Tertullian at the close of the second century AD. At first the term sacrament was connected loosely with all sacred doctrines, but later it became associated with only baptism and communion. The Roman Catholics added five more sacraments to the list: confirmation, penance, extreme unction, ordination, and matrimony.

When the Greek word *musterion* ("mystery") was translated into Latin, it occurred repeatedly as *sacramentum*. This translation was a misunderstanding of the Roman Latin word *sacramentum* and the Greek word *musterion* used by the apostle Paul. There is no evidence that Paul changed Christianity into a mystery religion and transformed the primitive rites into magical sacraments. Had Paul introduced baptism and communion as magical legal rites, his whole argument for a right relationship with God by faith in Christ would have been for nothing. His teaching of faith is ample proof that he did not accept ritual as a means of cleansing from sin or of obtaining benefits associated with salvation.

Sacraments are to be sure, useful signs for spiritual meditation and for the development of spiritual insight. However, the tendency to attach a magical significance to physical objects or words results in the interpretation of the sacraments that is deceitful, corrupting, and destructive of a genuine experience of God.

Protestants believe that their two sacraments, baptism and communion, are void of any magical content and are only signs and seals of the living faith. Roman Catholics affirm that the sacraments are *ex opere operato* and are necessary channels of divine grace.

While we do not believe that sacraments are essential channels for the transmission of God's grace, there is a tendency to apply magical notions to certain words. Many of these words are based upon the theology of a previous age. If proclaimers/ministers choose to use other words that more clearly explain these terms as they were meant to be in the Bible or try to relate them to modern-day expressions, many in the congregation may get the impression that it is not a religious service. The reason for this is that they have been so accustomed to hearing certain words to which they can relate, any innovation falls flat for them. We can only surmise from such a reaction that they have been geared to certain religious words that have a magical effect on them. They are worshiping God in the shadow of sacramental words.

I shall not enumerate all the words that have been used in a sacramental manner. Only a few will suffice. These are blood, justification, atonement, propitiation, redemption, and born again.

Blood

Numerous hymns contain references to the blood of Christ. With great gusto people sing them without really knowing to what blood refers. We have "There's Power in the Blood," "Alas and Did My Savior Bleed," "There Is a Fountain Filled with Blood," and "Nothing But the Blood."

The Old and New Testament writers did not wait for William Harvey of the seventeenth century to explain the circulation of the blood and its importance to the human body. They knew that the loss of blood meant the loss of strength, and from a mortal wound a person's life seemed to drain away. We say that blood is necessary for life, but the Hebrew people believed that life was in the blood. When the blood left the body, it carried the life with it. Furthermore, they affirmed that when the blood was shed, it still had a mysterious potency. This is why the Deuteronomic code prohibited the eating of blood. Because of the potency in blood even after it was shed, the Hebrews made elaborate provisions for the disposal of the blood of animals used in sacrifices. Blood was also used as a cleansing property to get rid of taboos so that one could worship God. Thus, when we use the analogy of blood with reference to Christ's death, we do so unaware of the meaning this held for the early Christians.

It appears that we make the analogy real, and it seems to be a reminder of the *Taurobolium* that was first used by the Magna Mater rites of Asia Minor in the first century AD and later performed by Mithraism. Over a platform, punctured with holes, a bull was slain. Under the platform stood a neophyte who bathed himself with the blood of the bull. From the blood the one initiated into the mystery cult received great strength. The rite performed a sacramental act in causing the initiated to be *renati in aeternum* ("born again into eternity").

Since blood meant life in biblical usage and since it had strange implications in the pagan world, it is much better to use life in our modern day. I cite two examples to illustrate.

In 1958 a New Testament professor published a book titled *Saved by His Life*. His title was drawn from a saying of Paul in Romans 5:10. In the book the author was critical of the hymns we sing that contain the themes of the blood of Christ. There was such an uproar among his denomination over this sensible approach that the professor was forced to resign.

Robert Bratcher, translator of *Good News for Modern Man*, once delivered a lecture at Furman University on his translation of the New Testament from Greek. All went well in the lecture until a woman in the session expressed her negative reaction in a very antagonistic manner. She denounced Bratcher fiercely for omitting the word "blood" in his translation and inserting the word "life." Evidently, blood conveyed a sacramental meaning. It seems that people have been hypnotized to respond to the word "blood," but if you give the sense of the term in its usage among early Christians, there is an angry reaction.

Justification

At the very outset allow me to say that I do not like the word "justification." It injects forensic notions into the teaching of Paul that were foreign to his mode of thought. The words "justify" and "justification" are Latin derivatives, and when used in connection with the action of God can imply that God as judge knows that we are guilty but makes a pronouncement of not guilty. This is a far cry from the Greek meaning of *dikaiosune* as used by Paul. It conveys the notion of a right relationship.

To a Jew in New Testament times the righteousness of God was more explicitly the righteousness of man. By observance of the commandments and doing good works, someone could be elevated to such great heights ethically that God was almost compelled to declare that person both accepted and acquitted. However, Paul perceived that this was all wrong (Rom 3:20, 28; 10:3; Phil 3:88ff). He did not understand the righteousness of God as an ethical quality that God possessed, nor did he think of it as a divine verdict of acquittal issued to people who were guilty. Rather, he saw it as an action of God in history bringing a person into a right relationship with himself. For Paul, the noun "righteousness" and the verb "to make right" were the same as "reconciliation" and "reconcile" (Rom 5:1, 9, 10).

Admittedly, there are places in Paul's letters where the word "righteous" is used in an ethical meaning, yet the main thrust of this word and its cognates is a relationship or a condition that now exists with God by faith in Christ. If we are interested in knowing what Paul thought about the ethical conduct of Christians, we gain this information not from his concept of righteousness, but from his teachings about union with Christ.

Atonement

The word "atonement" was coined by William Tyndale in his translation of the Greek New Testament. To him, atonement meant the making "at one" of those who were formerly alienated by enmity. Today atonement carries with it a sense of reparation, making amends, or giving satisfaction. It was only natural that the idea of reparation or satisfaction should become predominant in the word "atonement" with the prevalence of obnoxious theories of the death of Christ such as the payment of a ransom to the devil, punishment by God for human sin, and an act of God vindicating divine holiness and justice. In the King James Version, Romans 5:11 is the only place in the New Testament where the word "atonement" occurs. In the Revised Standard Version, "atonement" is substituted by "reconciliation."

Reconciliation is the establishment of friendly relations between parties who are at variance with each other, making peace after a rebellion has taken place against that one. When Paul spoke of reconciliation between a person and God, there was not the slightest indication that God had to change His attitude toward one. God was not angry at people. God did not demand that satisfaction be given by someone because His honor and dignity had been degraded by humanity, nor was there a necessity for a person to offer a sacrifice to placate God's hostility.

There was also no hint by Paul that the attitudes of God and humanity were mutually antagonistic. The hostility and estrangement had their origins in people. Through indifference, active enmity, and passive hatred, people had rebelled against God and stood in need of being reconciled to God. God was the subject of the action rather than the object. God took the initiative in breaking down the estranging barrier between God's self and humankind (2 Cor 5:18, 19; Rom 5:10).

Propitiation

The words "propitiation" or "expiation" have been translated from the Greek word *hilasterion*. The King James Version has "propitiation," whereas the Revised Standard Version has "expiation." Neither word is an adequate translation; both carry the sense of appeasement of an angry deity. William

Tyndale and Martin Luther, possibly in reaction to the Vulgate rendering of *hilasterion* by *propitiatorium,* followed the clue in Hebrews 9:15, the only other use of *hilasterion* in the New Testament, and translated the word properly as "mercy seat" (Luther, *Gnadenstuhl*).

In recent years there has been a return to an emphasis upon the meaning of *hilasterion* along with the attempt to set it more within the context of the ritual of the Day of Atonement. The importance of the mercy seat (*kapporeth*) in the religion of Israel was fully set forth in Exodus 25:17-22. It was at this place that God met with God's people through the high priest once each year in the ritual of the Day of Atonement. The high priest received a revelation from God that he was to impart to Israel. It seems clear that Paul was thinking in terms of a spiritual mercy seat—Christ—who was put forth publicly as a demonstration of God's activity in bringing humanity into a right relationship with God's self in contrast to the inaccessible, hidden, and hocus-pocus revelation found in the Levitical sacrificial system. According to the Apostle, God's mercy was supremely revealed in the crucified Christ, who is our mercy seat.

When many people hear the word "propitiation" or "expiation," a religious experience is extracted. However, when they hear the word "mercy seat," the correct word for what Christ has done, do they have the same kind of response? It is not likely. Therefore, propitiation and expiation become sacramental words apart from faith.

Redemption

The metaphors of deliverance in the Old and New Testaments, as is frequently the case in other religious languages, were drawn from the social systems and customs of the times.

The Hebrew and Greek words that have been translated into English as "redeem," "redemption," "redeemer," and "ransom" originally had to do with a price paid for the deliverance of a person from slavery, for securing a benefit, or for regaining possession of something that formerly belonged to a person. This notion of the payment of a price for release had almost lost this meaning in the Old and New Testaments, especially where the deliverance was an activity of God.

True, Paul did introduce money—payment in connection with the doctrine of deliverance—in two instances (1 Cor 6:20; 7:23). In both of these references he used the verb *agorazo* ("purchase") rather than *lutroo* ("release"), the usual word associated with deliverance. The context of 1 Corinthians 7:23 makes it quite apparent that the implied comparison is none other than a slave market. Paul conceived of believers as having been liberated from slavery by Christ. From these two passages and several others in the Pauline writings (Gal 3:13; 4:5; Eph 1:7; Rom 3:24; Col 1:14) the Church fathers formulated the first theory of atonement. Briefly put, this theory held that humanity was under the domination of Satan and that in order to liberate people, God offered Christ as a ransom to Satan. This kind of thinking plainly demonstrates what occurs when the dramatic language of Paul is reduced to prosaic literalism.

Romans 3:24 holds more interest for us in the consideration of the metaphor of redemption. In this verse, deliverance is joined with other concepts already present, for example, mercy seat and the righteousness of God. This deliverance effected through the death of Christ is defined in Romans as liberation from the powers of sin, from the wrath of God (the situation that pertains in life when people are alienated from God), from the law, and from the dominion and power of death. According to Paul, these were tyrannies that held humanity in check from which we must be freed. In Christ, completely beyond any merit or action on our part, we have come into a peaceful relationship with God and have been delivered from the slavery to powers of destruction.

In rabbinical circles during New Testament times, redemption was generally viewed as eschatological liberation. The redemption of Israel from Babylonian captivity had a forward reference to the nationalistic deliverance of Israel from its enemies. Paul believed that this release was already at work in Christ, but not in the nationalistic form of Jewish aspirations. Those who believed in Christ were the new Israel of God. They had received the Holy Spirit as a pledge of the greater eschatological liberation (Eph 4:30; Rom 8:23).

Born Again

Fundamentalist and conservative Christians today commonly use the term "born again." They use it in a redundant fashion with the word "Christian," saying they are "born-again Christians." Along with "blood," "born again" seems to have more sacramental or magic connotations than all the other words.

Those who emphasize "born again" as one of the chief catch-all phrases to describe true Christians depend upon Jesus' conversation with Nicodemus in John 3. Jesus said, "Except a man be born again, he cannot see the kingdom of God" (v. 3 KJV). It is customary for John to use a word with two meanings. Thus the word translated "again" (*anothen*) can be understood to be "from above" or "again." What Jesus was saying to Nicodemus was in a Jewish context. Jesus declared that unless he removed himself from legalism that sheltered him from a proper relationship with God, he was not submissive to the sovereignty of God (the kingdom of God.)

Instead of employing "born again," the apostle Paul said, "So if anyone is in Christ, there is a new creation: everything old has passed away; see, everything has become new" (2 Cor 5:17). The conversation with Nicodemus occurred before the resurrection of Jesus by which event he was declared Lord, the equivalent of the sacred name of God in the Old Testament, which was Yahweh. On the other hand, Paul used "new creation" for those who believed that Jesus had been raised from the dead and confessed him as Lord.

It appears that the Apostle refused to use the expression "born again" because he was aware of the "born again into eternity" upheld by the mystery cults of his time. He was also afraid that the pagan world would consider Christianity as another mystery cult. Paul certainly did not believe that words themselves mediated grace. Rather, for him, God's mercy is shown to us by God's revelation in Jesus Christ, and our response to that revelation is based strictly on our faith.

If we do not know the meaning of the words we use in our religious vocabulary, and if we refuse to accept a clear definition of the terms, then we believe that there is a certain magic in them and that they mediate grace. Therefore, we may worship God in the shadow of sacramental words.

Chapter 3

Glory of the Past
and Pessimism of the Future

The late William Lyon Phelps, professor of English literature at Yale University, once said, "We look backward
too much, and we look forward too much. Thus we
miss the passing moment." How true. We either look back to
a golden age of the past or forward to the utopia of the future.
Hitler and the Nazis glorified the heroic age of the German
people before Christianity was introduced to the German
tribes. Mussolini and the Fascists of Italy dreamed of reviving
the Roman empire of the past. We may glory in the past or
dream about the future, but what about the present age in
which we live?

Glory of the Past

In the Old Testament the Hebrew people constantly recalled
their liberation from slavery in the land of Egypt. They were
reminded of this event by the prophets and some of the
psalms. They also looked backward to the time when David
and Solomon were kings over Israel—in a sense, their golden
age. The tribes of Israel were united, the territory was
extended, the days were prosperous, the military force was
strong, and religion flourished. David conquered the Jebusites
and made Jerusalem the political and religious capital of the

tribes. He removed the tabernacle from Shiloh and took the ark of the covenant from the house of Obededom and transported them to Jerusalem. When Solomon succeeded his father as king of Israel, he arranged for the Temple to be built in the capital city.

This golden age of Israel was short-lived, however. When Solomon's son Rehoboam ascended the throne, he did not listen to the counsel of the old men, but took the advice of the young men. This was a grave mistake. The younger men advised him to be more severe in his demands on the people. When the people asked Rehoboam what his policy as king would be, he replied, "My father made your yoke heavy, but I will add to your yoke: my father disciplined you with whips, but I will discipline you with scorpions" (1 Kgs 12:14). Rehoboam's policy did not set well with the northern tribes, and the unified kingdom of David and Solomon came to an end. Israel of the north, constituting the majority of the tribes, went its own way, and the tribe of Judah and some of Benjamin were left high and dry. From that time on, prophets of Israel and Judah looked forward to the time when the tribes would again be united under a descendant of David. This person would be God's messiah ("anointed one") sent to deliver the Hebrew tribes from their enemies, bring peace and prosperity to the nation, and usher in the golden age of the past.

Similar to the Hebrews who looked forward to the coming messiah, some Christians today glory in the coming of the Holy Spirit on the day of Pentecost as recorded in Acts 2. They cry out, "What we need is a Pentecostal revival in our times." This was the ideal period of Christianity. If this were the ideal time, then we are limited in what we can do now. A cursory reading of Acts nullifies this assertion. In addition to external threats from the Jewish religious leaders, the fellowship of believers encountered many internal problems. The first blot on their reputation was an act of dishonesty perpetrated by

Ananias and Sapphira in Acts 5. Seeing that Barnabas got such a reputation for himself by selling his property and giving money to the apostles, Ananias and Sapphira desired similar praise. However, they sought the credit for giving all they had, but they kept a portion for themselves. They lied, and they died. If they had been able to accomplish their deceptive plan, it would have spelled doom for the early church. How could anyone believe their story that Christ had been raised from the dead if some of the fellowship lied?

Discrimination was another threat to the early Christian community. The Hellenistic Jewish Christian widows were not given their daily dole, or wages for subsistent living. Only those who were Palestinian Jewish Christian widows were included. Fortunately, the problem was solved by the selection of Hellenistic Jewish Christian men to administer the dole.

A third threat to the unity of the fellowship of believers arose when the disciples questioned how much of Judaism they were allowed to relinquish in order to be inclusive with the proclamation of the good news. Should they go to the Samaritans? Philip, a liberal Hellenistic Jewish Christian, did. Should they accept a eunuch? Philip told the good news to an Ethiopian eunuch. Should they eat with the Gentiles? Peter went to the house of Cornelius and proclaimed the gospel to his household and ate with them. Of course, there were repercussions. Peter's leadership position was downgraded after that incident. James, the brother of Jesus, became the leader. When the Christians in Antioch proclaimed the gospel to the Gentiles in Antioch in Syria, the church in Jerusalem sent Barnabas to check on the event and found that it was kosher. Then it was the apostle Paul who finally carried the good news to the Gentile world.

Far from being an ideal situation was the Pentecostal revival. This was the early stage of the Christian movement. If we have not advanced beyond this state, there seems to be little hope for Christianity. There are those who say, "Give me that old time religion," How old must it be? There are those who think the King James Version of the Bible is the only one that God blesses. We proclaim the final perseverance of the saints, when many do not have anything to persevere.

Some of the past actions of Christians haunt us today. During the Crusades in the Middle Ages, Christians under the guise of the banner of Christ killed women, old men, children, and babies of the Muslims. The mark of the Inquisition is also a horrible blot on Christianity. It was a disgraceful act to force pagans, Jews, and Muslims to become Christians.

In colonial Virginia, persons could be sent to jail for twice failing to attend church on Sunday. On a third offense they could be executed. Yet while these rules were in force, the slave trade went on with the blessing of the church. During the Industrial Revolution in England, many families were agitated when someone played the piano on Sunday, yet these same families made a profit from child labor.

Then there was the Salem witch hunt of the late seventeenth century when twenty witches were hanged and others were burned. The public mind was in a disturbed state, and blame was laid upon anyone who might do something that would classify as witchery. While Salem is known for its execution of witches, little is ever said about the witchcraft delusions prevalent all over Europe between the fourteenth and eighteenth centuries. During this time the witch fires were responsible for more than half a million deaths. From 1645 to 1647 one notorious witch-finder was responsible for sending three hundred witches to the gallows.

Over and beyond witch-hanging and burning is the institution of slavery upheld by our ancestors, who defended their actions because the South needed to raise cotton for the industries in the North. Even well-known ministers in the South used Scripture to prove that the institution of slavery was justifiable. Among the more notables were Richard Furman, founder of Furman University, and Basil Manley Jr., John A Broadus, and James Boyce, founders of the Southern Baptist Theological Seminary.

Yes, even in our country, Christian heritage has not always been on the side of Christian principles. While there was the declaration of freedom for all, the slaves did not experience it. Yet in their servitude they accepted the white man's God as the high God, who was above the animistic and polytheistic religion in Africa, who promised hope of liberation. To the American slaves we owe a debt of gratitude. Having little material wealth, they learned Christianity that came as crumbs from the master's table. In their chains of slavery and injustice they sang the great spirituals of hope and promise.

Perhaps our worship of God in the shadow of the glory of the past occurs because we fasten our attention on heroes of the faith of bygone days. The giants of yesteryear grow bigger each day with the food of our imagination until their size is tremendous. To be sure, in their day they made a great contribution to the Christian movement, but many of them had feet of clay. Some of them lived in a cultural environment that held them in check from expressing the high ideals of the Christian faith. Then too we must admit that they were merely human beings who possessed envy, jealousy, prejudice, and discrimination just as we do. Possibly we are dissatisfied with our own age of crime, dishonesty, drugs, wars and threats of war, injustices, distrust, denominational infighting, and the like, but let us not forget that we have greatly improved the horrible conditions that existed in what have been considered the "good old days." Minorities have been given their rights; women have shown their ability to be equal to men in all areas of life; an all-out effort is being made to curb crime; and more energy is being expended to opt for peace rather than war. Unfortunately, the only area where we see little improvement is in Christian circles. There are disagreements within communions over doctrines that have little significance in the ongoing of the Christian faith. Unfortunately, these internal conflicts lead nonbelievers to say to us, "Get your own house in order before you express your zeal in your witness to Christ."

Pessimism of the Future

Those who do not glory in the past and use it as a standard for ushering in a golden age in the present might be tempted instead to look to a utopia in the future. The word "utopia" is the combination of two words in the Greek *ou topos*, which means "no place." This future may be patterned after Sir Thomas Moore's *Utopia* or James Hilton's *Lost Horizon*. As we enter a new millennium, it seems that the direction is likely to move toward apocalyptic pessimism, of which there are many evidences.

Television programs are filled with horror movies, not the least of which dabble in apocalyptic thought. These include "Seventh Sign," "Millennium," and "Armageddon." The December 17, 1997 issue of *U.S. News and World Report* contained two articles about the apocalyptic fever of our times: "Dark Prophecies" written by Jeffery Sheler and "Lessons from Next-Year Country" written by Kathleen Norris. Sheler warned that apocalyptic imagery is everywhere. Examples included the amassing of weapons by the Branch Davidians in anticipation of the assault of demonic forces and the mass suicide by Heaven's Gate in an attempt to latch on to a comet in the termination of the age.

Other expressions of modern apocalyptic literature are the bestselling *Left Behind* series written by Tim LaHaye and Jerry Jenkins. By cashing in on the public's preoccupation with the year 2000, more than three million copies have already been sold. The series centers on the fundamentalist premillenarian view of the rapture in which Christ will return and take the righteous to heaven, and the wicked will be left to endure seven years of persecution. These books may be good horror stories, but they have little to do with sound and accurate biblical interpretation.

While books about the end of the age have appeared through the centuries, the impetus for this revival of interest stems from Hal Lindsey's sensational bestseller *The Late Great Planet Earth*, written twenty-five years ago. It is claimed that nearly 100 million copies have been sold throughout the world. In the 1990s other authors have pursued the path of Lindsey and written books of fiction or supposedly factual matters based on the books of Daniel or Revelation. Pat Robertson's *The End of the Age* is a fantastic and mind-boggling novel that borders on the ridiculous. To add to this are *The Coming Judgment of the Nations, Armageddon, Prince of Darkness, Final Warning*, and others written by Grant Jeffrey. Hopefully, the sales for these books have surmounted because of the horror interest and not because people take stock in any catastrophic event that may occur in the year 2000.

Instances can be cited from nearly every century since the first of mistaken predictors of the imminent end of the age. Among the contributors to this scheme of history are Montanus, Tertullian, Jerome, Cyprian, Gregory the Great, Bernard of Cluny, the Joachites, the Millerites, the Darbyites, the Irvingites, the British Israelites, the Jehovah's Witnesses, and finally some modern fundamentalists and some conservative Christians who hold a variety of premillenarian views. The chief sources for their calculations are the books of Daniel and Revelation. Presumably, these forecasters of future events have little knowledge of the basic tendencies of apocalyptic literature represented by these two books. Furthermore, they show no acquaintance with the noncanonical Jewish writings of the same genre. Thus they fail to understand the apocalyptic fixed calculations that proclaimed the future was then. Daniel and Revelation have become the happy hunting grounds to satisfy those who like to peer over the threshold of the yet-to-be.

It is a terrible mistake for people to call apocalyptic writings "prophecy." Those who designate Daniel as a prophet should be reminded that when the Jews canonized the Old Testament, they did not put Daniel with the Prophets section. It was relegated to the third section of the Hebrew canon under the title of Writings. Then, too, it is very clear that the book of Revelation is completely different from the other writings of the New Testament.

It is uncertain when and where apocalyptic literature received its label. Perhaps the name comes from *apokalupsis,* a Greek word used in Revelation 1:1. The word means to "uncover," "reveal," or "take the veil off." Since Revelation exhibited the characteristics of Daniel and the many noncanonical Jewish writings, the word "apocalypse" seemed to be appropriate for this literary type. This label is a misnomer, however. Quite frequently the apocalyptists put a veil on their teachings. They concealed rather than revealed.

How did the apocalyptists differ from the prophets of Israel? The prophets generally represented God's purpose in history, at least in part, as conditional on the people's conduct. Occasionally they foretold the future, but they affirmed that the actual events were dependent on what the people did. Thus the teaching of free will was one of the chief characteristics of their thought patterns. Both prophets and their successors, the Pharisees, were anxious to direct the will of the people in the direction of the will of God. The apocalyptists were determinists. They looked upon history as the working out of a predestined, unchangeable plan.

Keep in mind that the forte of the prophets was not prediction. Their predictions were not always fulfilled. In fact, Jeremiah was embarrassed because his predictions did not come to pass. He sharply accused God of letting him down. Also, the predictions of the prophets were unlike those of the apocalyptists. The prophets foretold the future that would arise out of the present, whereas the apocalyptists foretold the future that would break with the present. When the prophets saw sin and wickedness, they understood what the harvest would bring. In a sense they were ministers of doom, yet they did not speak only of doom. They could see with penetrating eyes through the darkness to a more distant future that gave glimpses of the glory that the righteous remnant would inherit when evil had consumed itself.

The apocalyptists had little faith in the present age to beget a brighter future. This is why they were called "pessimists." They looked for a great intervention of God to arrive in their own time. To the prophets, for the most part, the great empires of the world were merely instruments in God's hands to exercise his will on the faithless people of Israel. The apocalyptists viewed the great world empires as adversaries of God who proudly resisted God's will, but could not be successful. Rather, they would be annihilated. Certainly we cannot make too sharp a distinction here because there are some apocalyptic elements contained in a few prophetic oracles, but they are not dominant.

The prophets spoke from the standpoint of the present, whereas the apocalyptists retroceded into the past, assumed the name of some worthy person of the past recorded in the

Scriptures, and wrote as though that person gave the revelation. They believed there was more validity for an ancient revelation than there was for the new. The apocalyptists, under the guise of prophecy, recorded events of former years to set the stage for the great unfolding dénouement of history that was in their own time.

The prophets generally appealed to their listeners on the basis of reason and conscience, while the apocalyptists preyed upon the emotions and imaginations of the people. The apocalyptists received their revelation through intermediaries such as angels, visions, and dreams. They stressed the promises of God that they discovered through their avid study of Scripture, especially the prophets. On the other hand, the prophets came to the people announcing, "Thus says Yahweh" or the "The word of Yahweh came to me." Furthermore, they emphasized the necessity for the people to obey the commandments of Yahweh. The demands of God were clarified even more by the rabbis, not only by the written law, but also by the oral law that was codified by Jehuda Ha-Nasi around AD 200, known as the Mishnah.

This renewed apocalyptic fever epidemic keeps alive the old notions of Christians that we are just pilgrims on the way to a "land that is fairer than day." We sing, "This earth is not my home, I am only passing through," and "I am a stranger here within a foreign land; my home is far away upon a golden strand." We view earth as a place to endure while waiting for the return of Christ. Thus we sing, "Will Jesus Find Us Watching," "He Is Coming," "What If It Were Today," Lo, He Comes with Clouds Descending," "It May Be at Morn," and "The Lord Will Come." While these hymns remind us of the judgment to come, they also indicate a kind of paranoia, a fear and suspicion of the world around us. But herein is the contradiction. The more Christians fear the world and consider it something temporary, the more they imitate it.

We are not just followers of a remembered Christ or a coming Christ. He is the Christ of the past and future and of the here and now. It is easy to rush back two thousand years and confine Jesus to Palestine or in apocalyptic fashion to look to what is called "the second coming," but we must face the question, "Where is he now?" The author of the epistle to the Hebrews said, "Jesus Christ is the same yesterday and today and forever" (13:8). He is not an absentee or emeritus Christ. He is with us now and makes all the difference in the world.

In his earlier writings the apostle Paul thought that Christ would return in his own lifetime. In his later writings he seems to have moved away from this notion to accept the fact that Christ dwelt within him. Over and over again he used the phrase *en christo* ("in Christ").

John's Gospel alone records the farewell discourses of Jesus to his disciples. He does not attempt to remove the teaching of an end of the age and a judgment to come, but for him the second coming is the presence of the Paraclete (the Holy Spirit) who will confirm and carry forward the teaching of Jesus. Chapter 14 records Jesus' saying three times that he would come to his disciples (vv. 3, 18, 28) and one time that "we will come" (v. 23). Some have interpreted the coming of Jesus as a reference to the resurrection rather than the coming of the Spirit, although there is too close a relation in the discourse between Jesus' coming and the sending of the Paraclete to dissociate the two. The Paraclete will be the spiritual presence of Jesus (vv. 15-17); he will continue the work of Jesus; he will bear witness concerning Jesus (15:25-27); he will reprove the world concerning sin, righteousness, and judgment (16:8f); and he will guide the disciples to all truth (16:13). In chapter 15 where Jesus says that he is the vine and the disciples are the branches, and he will abide in the disciples and they in him, there is a close kinship to the mystical union of believer and Christ as taught by the apostle Paul with his "in Christ" formula.

It has been more than twenty-one hundred years since the first Jewish apocalyptists predicted the end of the age, which they thought would occur in their own lifetime. In fact, nineteen hundred years ago the Seer of Patmos expected the occurrence to be soon. About forty years earlier the apostle Paul believed that the termination of age was near. They were all mistaken. The future they contemplated was then. More years have intervened from the beginning of apocalypticism until our day than have intervened from the time of Abraham to the rise of apocalyptic literature. This fact should tell us something about modern-day predictions. Perhaps we should safeguard ourselves with a reverent silence about subject matter on which our predecessors felt cocksure. Those who are bedded down with the apocalyptic fever and cannot endure the tension between this-worldly and the other-worldly long for the consummation of history. The odds are possibly a billion to one that they will die before this happens. Therefore, it is incumbent upon us to live the Christian life and leave the rest to God.

There is always the danger of restricting our vision of Christianity to some point in time in the past and making it our goal for the present. However, we may discover that the "good old days" of our forebears were frequently frought with misconceptions, depersonalization of humanity, prejudice, hatred, jealousy, and discrimination. To be sure, there were those who were truly dedicated to God, but sometimes their voices were heard. Equally dangerous is the desire to set up a dream for the future whether it be a concentrated plan for church action or awaiting the action of God in history to overcome evil in the world. But what of the present? We draw from the past and anticipate the future, but it is in the now time that we live, move, and have our being.

Chapter 4

Tithing as a Legal Requirement

Giving is a very sensitive subject among people, even Christians, primarily because we are asked to contribute to a multitude of causes. Requests come through the mail or personal contacts to pledge funds to the United Way, the Red Cross, veterans groups, mental health agencies, the Cancer Society and other health agencies, homes for the aged, childrens homes, and denominational colleges and universities—to name a few. The list seems to be interminable. Even if we desire to make an offering, we can become so frustrated by the cries to donate to so many causes, we may shut out the pleas for contributions by becoming enclosed in a shell of indifference. Of course, it is impossible to donate to every fund-raising drive, no matter how worthy it may be. Thus we are forced to determine priorities in giving.

Most charitable agencies use gimmicks to achieve their fund-raising goals. Some of the attention-getting devices or features are frequently quite superficial. Many churches are chief offenders in their enthusiasm to raise the annual budget. Too often the tithe is the leverage utilized. Is this a deceptive or a genuine device? It remains for us to see whether tithing is used as a gimmick or as the proper way to contribute to the church. The only way we can be sure is to examine the teaching of tithing in the Old Testament and then turn to the New Testament to see if this plan of giving was continued.

Ministers commonly use the Old Testament passage of Malachi 3:8-10 to promote the tithe:

> Will a man rob God? Yet you are robbing me! But you say, "How are we robbing you?" In your tithes and offerings! You are cursed with a curse, for you are robbing me—the whole nation of you! Bring the full tithe into the store-house, so that there may be food in my house, and thus put me to the test, says the Lord of hosts; see if I will not open the windows of heaven for you and pour down for you an overflowing blessing.

Malachi was devoted to the temple and had an exalted view of the priesthood and its responsibilities. It is unknown whether he himself was a priest, yet he was such an advocate for the priesthood that he should be classified as a "cultic" prophet. He blamed the failure of crops in the land upon the refusal of the people to give the tithe. He believed that God withheld the rain that was essential for their agricultural life because the people omitted the tithe as an act of worship.

Prior to the time of Malachi, a tithe was kept in the towns every three years (Deut 14:28-29; 26:12-13). This tithe was for the benefit of the Levites, alien citizens, orphans, and widows. Do you ever hear of anyone citing these passages of Scripture in support of bringing the tithe into the church treasury? Of course not. They depend upon Malachi for chan-neling all funds to the church. If they used the Deuteronomic code, the total budget of the church would be restricted every three years to those who have no means of financial support. Who would be willing to accept this teaching?

The law of the tithe was instituted when Israel was an agricultural society. The farmers, cattle and sheep owners, vineyard keepers, and orchard tenders bore the brunt of the offerings in Israel. When a middle class arose, there was no provision made for tithing. Apparently the merchants, physicians, and other professional groups were exempt. This is why Jesus censured the Pharisees severely for scrupulously tithing garden condiments of anise, cummin, and mint (Matt 23:23). He condemned them for trying to fulfill the law with picky things rather than with their wealth and for omitting the weightier matters of the law such as justice, mercy, and faith. Now let us examine the teaching of the tithe in Judaism during the time of Jesus.

In the first century AD the majority of Jews lived outside the land of Palestine. Out of approximately 5,000,000 Jews who inhabited the world, at least 4,000,000 of those were scattered abroad in the Diaspora. Before the Hellenistic period, Jews lived in Babylonia, Persia, and Egypt. They represented the descendants of those who did not wish to return to Palestine when the opportunity was afforded them. After the conquest of Alexander the Great in the latter part of the fourth century BC, the Jews migrated to all parts of the known world. The majority of them moved west and settled in centers of Greek and Roman civilization, areas where they enjoyed greater freedom.

There is no evidence anywhere that the Diaspora Jews, those outside Palestine, ever gave a tithe of their income to the Temple in Jerusalem. They were subject to the temple tax, but beyond that they gave only as they voluntarily chose. Some volunteered to offer money for repairs to the Temple or for the Temple area. Alexander, the Alabarch of Alexandria, made a gift of gold-plated gates for the Temple area, the value of which was about a quarter of a million dollars. Alexander, the brother of Philo the Jewish Alexandrian philosopher, was perhaps one of the richest men in the world at that time.

The chief point to be stressed is that the Diaspora Jews were not under compulsion to tithe. They had to pay taxes in the land where they were either citizens or resident aliens. If the tithe was a requirement for the Palestinian Jews and not the Diaspora Jews, it becomes clear to us that the tithe was like an income tax. The religion of Israel and the state were one and the same. No distinction was made between civil matters and ecclesiastical matters.

Another reason why the tithe appears to be similar to an income tax is that it was abolished after the temple was destroyed in AD 70. It is true that the Mishnah is replete with references to the tithe, with the first division containing three tractates on the tithe. The same can be said of the various kinds of sacrifices, but these are recollections of the days when the Temple stood. In both cases we have an "as if" religion. It is the retention of acts of worship as if the Temple were still present. But these were retained only in the minds of the Jews.

There is nothing in the New Testament epistles to indicate that the Jewish tithing system was continued. It is to be noted that Paul's epistles were written before the fall of Jerusalem in AD 70. Some people will use 1 Corinthians 16:2 as an example of church giving and argue that the Apostle had in mind the tithe. They say that if you give as God has prospered you, it turns out to be a tithe. This is not what Paul meant. Verse 1 makes it clear that the contribution was intended for the poor saints in Jerusalem. The Apostle wanted the Christians in Corinth to lay aside an amount each week to be used as a part of the contributions from other churches. He planned to take the money to Jerusalem for the poor saints, with the hope that the gifts from the Gentile churches may cement better relations between Jewish and Gentile Christians.

When Paul made an all-out effort to aid the destitute Christians in Jerusalem, he never used the word "money" to describe the relief fund. He considered it to be:

• a fellowship (2 Cor 8:4; 9:13; Rom 15:16)
• a ministry of service (2 Cor 8:4; 9:1, 12, 13)
• a grace (2 Cor 8:4, 6, 7, 19)
• a bounty or liberal gift (2 Cor 8:20)
• a blessing (2 Cor 9:5)
• a service of worship (2 Cor 9:12)
• a collection (1 Cor 16:1)
• alms (Acts 24:17)

Of these terms, "grace" is the most expressive of the Christian faith. Here, giving is a grace—not a duty or an obligation. Wherever there is a display of the grace of God in the community of believers, we witness an inborn zeal to return to others the gracious love of God. The grace of giving provides food for the hungry, a home for the homeless, clothes for the naked, defense for the oppressed, and health for the sick.

In 2 Corinthians 8 Paul gives two examples of the proper motive for giving: the Macedonian Christians and the supreme precedent set forth by Christ. The Apostle used the Macedonian Christians, who had given generously to the relief fund, as an example to the church in Corinth whose members had made a pledge, but did not come through with the collection. The Macedonians contributed not only according to their ability, but also beyond their ability. Their donation was not based on pressure tactics, but on their own free choice. They begged for the privilege of sharing in the love gift. The believers from Macedonia would not permit the aloofness of the Jewish Christians in Jerusalem or their hostility toward Gentile believers to restrain them from lending a helping hand. What they contributed was beyond expectation because the people were so poor that Paul declined to ask them to participate. First and foremost they gave themselves in complete commitment to Christ. They demonstrated that the grace of giving is to give oneself first and then offer substance.

In 2 Corinthians 8:9 Paul presents Christ as the ultimate example of giving. In verse 8 he notes that love must manifest itself in generous action, which led Paul to emphasize that his real motives for giving were Christ's example and his gratitude to Christ for his involvement in behalf of sinners. The unmerited favor, love, and mercy that Christ bestowed on us were costly. He became poor by entering the lowly state of humanity, allowing himself to be buffeted, humiliated, and despised. He laid aside his glory to assume the form of a servant. The purpose of his willing submission to a humble career was in our behalf. It was to enable humanity to become rich with the meaning of life.

Tithing was not made a requirement by the Christian fellowship until the fourth century AD. It was only after an ecclesiastical establishment was set in motion that the Christian priest was said to be analogous to the Jewish priest or Levite. This status naturally carried with it the requirement of the tithe similar to Judaism. The Council of Macon in AD 585 decreed the payment of tithes to the church, and those who did not comply were to be excommunicated. Yet there were those who refused to abide by this decree and said that tithing was no more binding for Christians than was circumcision.

Clearly, our situation is unlike the situation that pertained to the Jews in the Old Testament. Their tithe was similar to an income tax because the religious congregation and the state were one. We have a split stewardship. We are obligated to the government for the income tax, and to that is added the need for money to carry out the witness to Christ in the world.

Too often we forget that some of the money we give for income taxes is also used for religious services. Protestants, Catholics, Jews, and Muslims alike benefit from the national coffer. Millions of dollars are spent for the salaries of chaplains in veterans hospitals and for military chaplains, chapels, chapel equipment, religious education directors, and the like. Are we not, in fact, getting a free ride from the government in this mission work? It has been suggested that churches pay for the support of chaplains in the military. However, there are two disadvantages to this arrangement. First, it is unlikely that many churches would be willing to lend their support. Second, if chaplains were considered ordinary civilians without rank as officers, they would have very little to say in the chain of command.

In the August 15, 1998 issue of the *Greenville News* there was an article about the Evangelical Council for Financial Accountability, an association of Christians who are interested in religious financial planning. One of the members interviewed said that part of being a Christian is giving to the church. He said, "When I first started, I knew that a Christian ought to give a tithe to the church. I got my pencil out and figured it out, but I could not pay it." But he went on to say that this did not stop him. He began to give ten percent to the church. He ended his testimony by saying, "The fourth week I may have had a can of beans, but it worked."

The forte of some Christian churches has been the enthusiastic support of the tithe as the minimum requirement for Christian giving. Anything above this amount is considered an offering. In spite of legalistic hammer blows that resound from the pulpit, it would be interesting to know how many members of these churches actually tithe. I have no problem with those who decide on a tenth for their share in stewardship, but I resent anyone who imposes this legalism on others.

When I finished high school during the depression years, my parents did not have the money to send me to college. Fortunately, I was able to get a job in a paper mill located in North Louisiana. My pastor in my hometown was very zealous in pushing the tithe as a minimum for giving. In fact, he stressed the tithe so much that he gave me guilt feelings for not tithing. If I had known then what I know now, there would have been no problem. My job gave me the opportunity to save money for my college education as a ministerial student. Since the priests of the Old Testament were exempt from the tithe but were paid by the tithes of others, as a prospective ministerial student, I could have claimed exemption, and my guilt feelings would have been removed. Every two or three weeks I would get out on the highway and try to hitch a ride to my hometown. Whenever it was difficult to catch a ride, my thoughts turned toward tithing, and I made a vow to God that if He would help me get a ride, then like Jacob of old I would say, "All that you give me I will surely give one tenth to you" (Gen 28:22). I came to realize that this was nothing more than trying to bargain with God, a loyalty of the lowest level.

When I entered Louisiana College, the matter of giving a tenth was still a vexing problem for me. It was not long before tithing was presented to me as a backwash of Jewish legalism. This understanding came to me through Paul Stagg, who was a junior when I was a freshman. Through the insights he gave me I perceived that tithing was not the way for true stewardship in giving.

After completing my doctoral degree, a large church congregation asked me to become their interim pastor. The time came when I was supposed to preach a sermon on stewardship because the budget was presented. Should I preach about tithing or not? I selected the "not" option. In the sermon I stated that tithing was unfair and gave the reasons why. The church in previous years had never pledged the budget under the compulsory tithe system. That year the people pledged thirty percent more than the previous year. What happened? Some of the members of the congregation told me later that they could not give a tenth, and since they felt that they were already guilty of sin, they had given nothing in previous years. In the sermon I had said that one should give as much as possible, which members were willing to do.

Let us now take a quick look at the unfairness of tithing. (1) A widow receives about $1,000 a month from Social Security for the support of four children. She is able to work part-time and add to that amount about $500 a month. Her family's total is $1,500. Should she give $150 a month? Absolutely not. To be sure, if she wants to give that amount, it remains her decision. She has to consider whether or not she is able to do this in the light of her total outlay for all expenses during the month. However, no one should press her into thinking she is under compulsion to do so. (2) A single person makes $5,000 a month. He decides to tithe the income and give $500 a month. Are we to believe that the $500 the single person gives is on an equal basis with the $150 the widow gives? The single person does not have four children to support, and look at the amount he has left over even after income taxes have been withheld.

Several other techniques are used to pressure people into giving to the church. We are promised that we will receive more wealth if we tithe. This may be a good business deal, but it has little to do with Christian commitment. It may make sense as an investment, but not for church stewardship. Some take this gimmick and run with it. They say, "God, I will give you money provided you give me more in return." In fact, there are those who brag about their prosperity as having come by this means. This approach is nothing more than a bribe.

You have heard it said, "If you give a tenth, the remainder will go farther in your support." This, too, is nothing more than a business deal. It is related to the device of obligation. Thus, stewardship is considered a tribute to God. Just as the landowner expects a cut of the crop from his tenant, so God demands a tribute. It is true that we are indebted to God, but should our stewardship be based on a sense of duty—a debtor paying dues to a worthy creditor?

The highest incentive for stewardship should be the presentation of our offerings out of gratitude for what God has graciously done for us. My wife and I have always contributed to the Christian fellowship because we count it a privilege to do so, not as a means to gain God's favor or out of a sense of duty. Instead of counting our blessings, as some people hope for by giving their offerings, we want to make our blessings count.

One other thing should be called to our attention about stewardship. When we contribute to the church, we are responsible for the way the money is used. Some members give and say they are not responsible for what is done with their offering. They are mistaken. If they are responsible for contributing, they have the added responsibility of knowing where the money goes.

There is a distinct advantage in promoting the tithe. It makes giving a priority among Christians and affords a specific plan for giving. This takes it out of the nickel-and-dime category, but there is a danger of the acceptance of tithing as a rule rather than as a privilege. When we recognize our stewardship as a privilege, we are not bound by legalism. Rather, we are open to a love that prompts us to make a greater offering than the tithe.

Chapter 5

Manipulation and Admiration

The Israelites tried to manipulate God with the ark of the covenant in the days of the judges. They thought if they took the ark into battle against their enemies, they were assured of victory. In like manner they felt secure in Jerusalem against the invasion of their enemies because God's presence was in the Temple. Furthermore, they believed that through the sacrifices offered to God, their protection was assured. Some even tried to manipulate God by appealing to God to show divine superiority over the gods of the surrounding nations. All of these methods failed to form a protective shield, however.

Along with their attempts to manipulate God, the Israelites attempted to win God's approval with praise and admiration. But with all of their admiration, the majesty of God was not increased one bit. Do Christians try the same ploys as the Hebrew people did to get God on their side?

Manipulation

Christianity in our country is no longer an accessory; it has become a standard operating procedure. Few politicians would run for office unless they were affiliated with some Protestant or Catholic communion. We open and close sessions at political conventions with a prayer. The U.S. Congress and some state legislatures employ chaplains. Witnesses in a court of law are required to swear by the name of God that they are telling the truth. There is a presidential prayer group that meets occasionally in Washington, D.C. The Boy Scouts of America have God and country in their oath, and they present the God and Country award. "Under God" has been added to the pledge of allegiance. "In God We Trust" is stamped on our coins and greenbacks. Our government has military chaplains. On the surface all of these things are good, but the question is: "Does God control us, or do we try to control God?"

All idolatry begins with our desire to control our deity. Isaiah 46 denounces the idolatry of the Babylonians. The prophet probably referred to the New Year's festival procession in Babylon. The worshipers of Bel-Marduk and Nabu carried the idols of these gods on beasts that crumpled under their weight. Isaiah demonstrated the weaknesses of the gods that the Babylonians made with their hands and carried around on beasts to affirm that the God of Israel was the God of the universe.

Pagan worship was also evident in the early days of Christianity. The apostle Paul in Romans 1:18-32 gives us a picture of the pagan society of his day. The pagans were under the wrath of God, the situation that pertains when people are alienated from God. The pagans had taken the invisible nature of deity, clearly perceived in creation, and changed it for images resembling humans, birds, animals, or reptiles. They exchanged the truth about God for a lie and worshiped the creature rather than the Creator. For this reason God allowed the pagans to pursue their own way, which ended up in all sorts of sinful acts.

We abhor idols and wonder how persons of the past could have brought themselves to the position of bowing down to a god made of wood, stone, or metal. Gods have no power.

They are as inept as the ones who manufacture them. But the motive of those who construct idols is to control their deity.

While we may not make idols with our hands, is it possible that we produce idols in our minds? The philosopher Voltaire once said, "God created man in his own image, and man has returned the compliment." Do we use God in the same way Aladdin in *Arabian Nights* wielded the magic lamp and ring to call up a genie to do his bidding? Do we subscribe to a tailor-made deity to suit our own interests? There is a tendency for some to accept what is useful about God but refuse to submit to God's demands. Others reduce God to size and make God play lacky to their questions, answering them in accordance to their own answers. Still others may resort to making God dance to their tune, meet their time schedule, and come to their beck and call to promote schemes that are contrary to God's character. It is so easy to call upon God to jump in and fix things when we have messed up. However, we must remember that God does not bless our stupidity.

If we try to make a genie out of God, we become estranged from God. Thus the God of the universe becomes a reflection of ourselves. Frequently, Christians will try to manipulate God in order to lubricate the clashing gears of society, give peace of mind to the anxious and a quiet spirit to the troubled and worried, send a sense of belonging to the lonely, and promise success to those who are starting out in life. Some of these things do occur through faith in Christ, but simply using the Christian faith for these ends is a type of profanity.

Some of the most atrocious crimes, shameful acts, cruel injustices, and evil schemes have been committed under the spell of certain magic words and phrases—not the least of which is "the will of God." Bloody wars have been waged under the banner of God's will. Many injustices and sins have been upheld by those who led others into the belief that they were in harmony with God's intention. When other incentives fail in promoting a program, a religious leader will occasionally fall back on the slogan that has been successful in the past: "It is the will of God that we do this." God's name may have been blasphemed more by those who claim God's approval for something they desire than by those who openly profane God's name in cursing.

How do we know the will of God? Some arrive at a decision very quickly. They suppose that God approves of their self-interest in making the decision. They do not permit the character of God revealed in Jesus Christ to be the criterion of their choice. Usually, Christians seek support in their own preconceived notions or attempt to give a false interpretation of Scripture.

The first step toward knowing God's will is to have a personal relationship with God by faith in Christ. From that experience we move to the study of Scripture for an understanding of the character of God. This determines whether or not what we intend to do is consistent with our knowledge of God's character. In times past if persons wished to know the will of God, they had to obey the king because on the basis of his divine right he gave the voice of God. Until the Reformation, uncritical obedience was given to the pope, priest, or church council. Even today in some churches the pastor is looked upon as the one who knows the will of God. Can we trust an individual to have a clear-cut knowledge of the intention of God? Or can we place confidence in the cumulative voice of the majority to determine the voice of God? The free person in Christ cannot delegate his or her conscience to a ruler, a pastor, a pope, or a group of people. Each person stands alone before God and is aided in decision making by the fellowship of the saints of all ages.

Since World War II, Christian communions have rallied around particular issues that appear to be more political than religious. Among these issues are abortion, homosexuality, prayer in public schools, and equal rights for African Americans and women. Those who have twisted the gospel of love into a gospel of hate have violently opposed abortion and the rights of homosexuals, African Americans, and women even to the point of murder.

The same group believes it is the will of God that prayer should be included as part of the public school program. Have they been misled to believe that students are unable to pray anywhere at any time? Students have the privilege of organizing prayer groups on school grounds provided that the time given for this spiritual exercise does not interfere with the education program. These protagonists want much more, however. They advocate a structured prayer that becomes a requirement for all students—Protestants, Catholics, Jews, Muslims, and so on. There are others who opt for a time set aside for voluntary prayer. This view also has its problem. What if some students out of their religious conscience decline to pray? The other students will look upon them as strange or atheists. Why use the gospel of love to stir up animosity? Then, too, why is it so necessary to parade before others one's piety in an institution that is not geared for religious services? Persons can pray at home or at church, thereby avoiding the desire to make a show of their faith.

Jesus warned us of two dangers to avoid as we pray to God: arrogance and ignorance. The motive of some Pharisees in praying was to be seen by people. They wanted to be praised for their piety. But such persons deceived themselves and others. Especially dangerous was the repetition of words similar to pagan usage. They thought that the repetition of meaningless phrases contained the power to manipulate their gods. If they prayed long enough, they believed, they could force the gods to comply by exhausting them. There are occasions when Christians try to manipulate members of the church in their attempt to manipulate God. If some are unable to sway others by their schemes, projects, or concoctions, they will say, "Let us pray about this and seek God's will." If the intention is good and well-meaning, the request is proper and fitting. Too often, however, the motive is a pressure tactic to get the members to conform.

Posture, place, and time do not set the pace for prayer, but the ability to remove ourselves from hindrances and obstruction to worship does matter. It is possible to pray while sitting at a desk, riding in a car, mowing the lawn, washing the car, cooking a meal, or vacuuming the floors. As Bernard of Clairvaux said in one of his sermons,

> Whoever with prayer and diligent devotion is watchful towards the spiritual world will depart hence safely and be received into the world with great joy. Wherever, therefore, thou shalt be, pray secretly within thyself . . . If thou shalt be in bed, or in any other place, pray there; thy temple is there.

It is not that people try to live without God, though some do. Rather, they want God on their own terms. Martin Luther, as an Augustinian monk, not only submitted to the rigorous disciplines of his order, but he also imposed upon himself self-denials to gain the favor of God. It was only after he had climbed by these means to gain God's acceptance and found that success resulted in greater depths of despair that he was ready for the illuminating alternative—grace. There are persons who do not climb as high as Luther to gain God's favor, but they settle with the illusion that they have arrived. They whittle God down for size, and with priggish pride, moral mediocrity, and spiritual smugness they are paralyzed by the mirage of righteousness. They are like those to whom Paul alluded when he said, "They have a zeal for God, but it is not enlightened. For, being ignorant of the righteousness that comes from God, and seeking to establish their own, they have not submitted to God's righteousness" (Rom 10:2-3).

How are we to curb ourselves from manipulating and using God for our own designs and objectives? We must remember that God is creator and sustainer of the universe, that God is God and not man. God does not bear the image of man, but man bears the image of God. We must remember that while God is with us, God is also transcendent. God's thoughts are not our thoughts; God's ways are not our ways.

We noted in the introduction that both manipulation and admiration are attempts to control God. Let us now examine admiration as a shadow of worship.

Admiration

Thomas Carlyle, the famous Scottish essayist and historian, was invited to attend a small literary guild in England. A woman of high social rank made a speech in which she denounced the Jews for rejecting Christ. She ended her diatribe by expressing her regrets that Jesus did not appear in her own time. She said, "I would have been delighted to receive him into my home and listen attentively to his teachings." Turning to Thomas Carlyle, she exclaimed, "Don't you think so, Mr. Carlyle." Carlyle responded, "No, Madam. I don't. I think that had he come very fashionably dressed with plenty of money and preaching the doctrines suitable and palatable for the higher estates, I might have received from you a card of invitation on the back of which would have been written, 'To meet our Savior.' But if he had come as he did come uttering his sublime precepts and denouncing the Pharisees and associating with publicans and the lower orders, you would have treated him as the Jews did. You would have cried out, 'Take him out to Newgate and hang him.' "

If we had been present in the time of Jesus' ministry and had accepted the Pharisees' interpretation of the Law and the oral tradition with which they surround the Law, doubtless, we would have joined the religious leaders with cries of "Crucify him, crucify him!" No, admiration is not enough, especially when the high esteem is pushed back hundreds of years before the influence of Christ made an indelible impression upon history. To the religious leaders and some of the populace Jesus was considered a troublemaker. Indeed, he was the most disturbing personality to appear in history. His parables were like lightning bolts from the blue. They shocked the listeners out of their complacency.

Joseph Addison said, "Admiration is a very short-lived passion that immediately decays upon growing familiar with its object."[1] Praise and admiration can be evasions of commitment. To claim that Jesus was the greatest teacher who ever lived is not of itself a commitment. A person should go beyond adulation to an experience with Christ by faith.

Philips Brooks, the rector of Trinity Church in Boston during the latter part of the nineteenth century who composed the hymn "O Little Town of Bethlehem," told this story about a missionary from Africa who was on furlough: The missionary purchased a sundial so that he could tell the time of day. When he returned to Africa, he put the sundial in the middle of the African village. The villagers admired it so much that they put a roof over it to protect it from the sun and rain. Of course, the roof kept the sundial from functioning.

Christ came to tell us of things more important than the time of day, yet there are those who become so infatuated with his teachings, deeds, convictions, and manner of life that they have sheltered themselves from a commitment to him.

There is no doubt in my mind that Judas Iscariot admired Jesus. He and Jesus did not see eye to eye on the mission of Jesus. Judas was a zealot and wanted to use Jesus as a firebrand for a political revolution. Yet his admiration for Jesus did not save him from spiritual ruin. Before he killed himself he saw the error of his ways and confessed that he had betrayed innocent blood. Judas is still alive and kicking. Jesus is being sold for a popular conception of Christianity. Surely Judas heard the words of Jesus: "Blessed are the peacemakers," "Love your enemies," "Pray for those who persecute you," and "Blessed are the merciful." He saw Jesus comfort people, associate with the outcasts of society, show concern for the poor, give sight to the blind, and heal the sick and diseased. Judas has become a byword in the Christian tradition. We hold him in contempt. No one would dare name a son Judas. We use his name when someone betrays a confidence or sells out to the opposition. Nevertheless, we brand ourselves as traitors to a divine trust if our relationship is based solely on the level of admiration.

In 1939 Orson Welles portrayed on radio as an actual happening H. G. Wells' *War of the Worlds*, a story of an imagined invasion from Mars. At the time I was a seminary student living in Louisville, Kentucky. When I heard the broadcast on my radio, I vacillated between belief and unbelief with respect to the reality of the event. It was reported that neither Welles nor CBS had any notion that listeners would believe it was a real invasion. But they did. After the incident caused a wide range of fear among those who listened, H. G. Wells sharply critized Orson Welles for taking the story and removing it from its location. He changed fiction into reality. This is what admiration can do for us. It is possible for us to retreat to the first century AD and praise the life, works, and teachings of

Jesus but never put them on location for today. If Christ is enshrined in the dead past of two thousand years ago in the land of Palestine, he does not reach us today.

An enlisted man said to a Navy chaplain, "Chaplain, I wish to God that I had lived back when Jesus was on earth. I have tried to pray to God, but He is not real to me. By that I mean He is not as real as my shipmates, my mother, my father, or my girlfriend. Back in Palestine I could have gone to Jesus and knelt down, looked into his face, heard his voice, felt him reach out and touch me. Chaplain, I feel under these conditions I could have been a better fellow."

It seems that the enlisted man in this story could not relate to the Christ who is with us today. He was more interested in the historical Jesus who lived and moved among the early disciples, the Jesus who healed, taught, and loved those who came to see and hear him. His mind was set on the Jesus of long ago, not on the one who is present with us today.

For many years I have been deeply moved by James Russell Lowell's poem "The Vision of Sir Launfal." The poem tells of a knight, clad in shining armor and mounted on a spirited charger, leaving his castle on a beautiful summer morning. He goes forth in search of the Holy Grail, the cup from which Jesus drank at the Last Supper. As the knight passes through the castle gate, the horrible sight of a leper throws a dark shadow over his noble adventure. In disdain he tosses a coin to the leper. The leper refuses to pick up the coin because it is given out of a sense of duty and because he considers it a handout rather than as a gift to share in his pain. The knight travels for many years through many lands. Finally, penniless and weary of his journey, he decides to return without having achieved his goal. At Christmas he arrives at a brook, and there he sees the leper who sat at the castle gate when he began his adventure. His vision is no longer downward, but on a level with the beggar. This time he shares a moldy brown crust of bread with the leper and gives him a drink of water in a wooden bowl. Suddenly the leper becomes Christ, and the bowl becomes the Holy Grail. The leper, who is now Christ, remarks:

> The Holy Supper is kept, indeed,
> In whatso we share with another's need;
> Not what we give, but what we share,
> For the gift without the giver is bare;
> Who gives himself with his alms feeds three,
> Himself, his hungering neighbor, and me.[2]

In his veneration of a relic of the past, the knight at the outset of his journey missed the opportunity of confronting the living Christ when he showed contempt for the leper. At the end his admiration was exchanged for an experience with Christ. This poem reminds me of the parable of the separation of the sheep and the goats in Matthew 25:31-46. When the righteous were surprised by the commendation of Christ, they replied, "Lord, when was it that we saw you hungry and gave you food, or thirsty and gave you something to drink? And when was it that we saw you a stranger and welcomed you, or naked and gave you clothing? And when was it that we saw you sick or in prison and visited you?" Christ replied, "Truly I tell you, just as you did it to one of the least of these who are members of my family, you did it to me" (vv. 37-40).

It is possible for us to admire and love God abstractly, dissociated from any particular instance. Thus, admiration ends up as theory without any factual basis. Jesus, quoting from the Old Testament Law, said that we are to love God with our whole personality and love our neighbor as ourselves.

Notes

[1]Robert Shafer, *From Beowulf to Thomas Hardy*, vol. 2 (Madison WI: Odyssey Press, 1944) 709.

[2]James Russell Lowell, *Poetical Words* (Boston: Houghton, Mifflin & Co., 1885) 122.

Chapter 6

Familiarity, Secondhand Religion,
and a Last Resort

There are three shadows that are presumptive in nature. One is familiarity of religious experience. Our busy round of activities within the Christian community can become so presumptuous that our commitment to Christ becomes humdrum and monotonous. The shadow of a secondhand religion is based on the assumption that one is a Christian, but in reality the faith is a borrowed experience from someone else. The shadow of a last resort takes for granted that God will come to the rescue in time of need, whether or not a vital relationship is maintained.

Familiarity

The Pharisees were the religious experts of Judaism in the first century. Numbering about 6,000, they were the most religious men who ever lived. Because they were very conscientious about observing the Law, they accumulated minute regulations to bind the people to the Law. For example, the Pharisees specified how far people were allowed to travel on the Sabbath, and they made picky distinctions between clean and unclean. While most of these religious authorities were quite sincere, when Jesus visited the synagogue in Nazareth, he encountered insincerity and suspicion from them.

Luke gives more details about Jesus' appearance in his hometown than do Mark and Matthew. According to Luke, Jesus went to the synagogue on the Sabbath. Apparently the *chazzan*, the synagogue attendant, gave Jesus the scroll of Isaiah to read as the *haftarah* for that day. Jesus unrolled the scroll and read from Isaiah 58:6 and 61:1-2.

> The spirit of the Lord God is upon me, because the Lord has anointed me; he has sent me to bring good news to the poor. He has sent me to proclaim release to the captives and recovery of sight to the blind, to let the oppressed go free, to proclaim the year of the Lord's favor. (Luke 4:18-19)

After reading these verses Jesus rolled up the scroll, gave it back to the *chazzan*, and sat down. In his comments on the scripture passage he said, "Today this scripture has been fulfilled in your hearing" (v. 21).

Members of the synagogue, some of whom were Pharisees, exclaimed, "Is not this Joseph's son?" (v. 22b). Matthew and Mark add son of Mary; his brothers James, Joseph, Simon, and Judas; and his sisters (Matt 13:55-56; Mark 6:3). At first the Pharisees were amazed at what Jesus said, but their amazement faded into hostility when Jesus introduced Elijah and Elisha who ministered to Gentiles. God was there in their midst, and those who were so familiar with the Jewish religion wanted to get rid of Him.

There is an old adage that says, "Familiarity breeds contempt." We can become so accustomed to something that we grow estranged from it. Martin Luther once said, "I will say one thing boldly and freely. Nobody in this life is nearer to God than those who hate and deny Him. And He has no more dear children than these." This statement from Luther may strike us as strange and shocking, but as we reflect on it, we recognize that considerable truth is contained in it. Concerned unbelievers who hate or disclaim God may be misguided individuals, but at least they take God seriously. They do not take God for granted as do some believers whose faith has become so familiar to them that it breeds contempt.

At the moment Christ died, nothing could have been more doomed to extinction than the movement he founded. There were comparatively few disciples; and one of them denied him, and another betrayed him. The early disciples could claim no meeting place of their own. If they spoke in their own tongue, Aramaic, it was recognized as a quaint dialect. So insignificant was the movement that it would have been foolish partiality to have predicted anything other than a limited existence as a Galilean sect. How could these uneducated disciples, scandalized by a leader who was put to death on a cross like a common criminal, survive in a world filled with many ways of salvation? But they did survive and turned the world upside down. After many years the church settled into complacency, and instead of living and proclaiming their faith, they sank into a lazy glow of orthodoxy that stifled their zeal. When God became too familiar to them, they took God for granted.

Likewise, in our own lives certain events and activities can keep us from taking God seriously. For example: Routine activities of the church such as committee work, formulating programs, and pledging the budget are all necessary, but they should not sidetrack us in our worship of God. A break in the family circle can bring pangs of loneliness, but it has the power to remind us of the presence of one in the household whom we took for granted. A collapse in a business venture may bring hardship to our family, but it may also cause us to see favorable factors and elevate the issue of making a life rather than making a living. A loss of health may take us out of the stream of activity, but it shows what the real current of life is. As we slide into the routine of unheroic sameness in the church, we need some bolt from out of the blue to shake us to our foundation where it may be possible to distinguish between what is relevant and irrelevant, what is temporal and eternal, and what is spiritual and worldly.

Now let us consider the second presumptive shadow, secondhand religion.

Secondhand Religion

Some people who call themselves Christians have never had an experience with God through faith in Jesus Christ. They live on the faith of others who are spiritually minded. Their religion is hearsay. It is based upon the witness of someone in whom they trust. For example, through association with a sincere and dedicated pastor, they may come to view Christianity as something real. Therefore, they trust in the pastor and not in Christ. Or a faithful friend or devoted parents may cause them to make a confession of faith. Like Peter Pan, who never grew up, these "secondhand believers" never mature in the faith because they began with a secondhand religion.

Physical growth is normal, steady, and sure. Yet in the arena of the spiritual, growth is not always certain. Spiritual maturity involves the ability to think objectively about ourselves, to cultivate the habit of an open mind, and to devote ourselves to living in a right relationship with God and others.

Persons who do not mature in the faith live off the faith of others because they never began in faith. In mass evangelism the majority of those who come forward to confess faith in Christ are repeaters. They made a confession in years past, but the experience was secondhand. This is why they are under compulsion to begin all over again. There is the impression that their secondhand religion was unable to carry them through life. Little did they realize that the Christian life is not dependent on a first fling of faith based on the faith of someone else. Rather, a personal faith in Christ begins in faith and continues in faith (Rom 1:17).

It is extremely difficult for someone who has a secondhand religion to be a witness to the good news of God reconciling the world to God's self in Christ. The English word "witness" comes from the Anglo-Saxon word *witan*, which means "to know." The Greek word from which the English translation was made means the same. To be a witness, a person must have experienced something, if the testimony is to be reliable. The sense of reality, a conviction that dominated the early disciples, was not transmitted as belief of someone else. It was a possession that could not be destroyed. They did not have to make repeated confessions, as some do in today's revivals. The sense of reality came to them because they knew that the historical Jesus who moved among them had been raised from the dead. Since only God had power over life and death, through Christ's death and subsequent resurrection, they were able to confess Jesus as Lord (Yahweh) of the Old Testament (Phil 2:5-11). With a secondhand religion a witness can do nothing more than refer the person to someone who has a firsthand religion.

Many years ago I was traveling by car to Roanoke, Virginia. When I neared Charleston, West Virginia, a tire went flat. I had no spare tire, and nightfall was approaching. About a half mile up the road was a service station. I removed the flat tire and lugged it to the service station. The manager of the station reluctantly agreed to fix it, but he let me know in no uncertain terms that he really did not have time to fix the flat because it was late, and he had promised his wife that he would take her to a "damn prayer meeting." From his conversation I could tell right off that his religion was secondhand. His faith was his wife's faith.

In a secondhand religion, persons live on the edges of life. They may come to the fellowship of the saints once in a while. It is a sort of social call on God. The individuals leave a calling card lest God be encountered, but in leaving the card it is hoped that someone will report to God that they were there. On the fringes they can do as they please. Intermittently, money is given as a kind of voluntary tax with the hope that God will never see the accounts. In a secondhand religion, when something has to be done, these persons will beg off because of lack of talents. Their competency level is out of the comfort zone.

John Newton, a great English singer and powerful preacher of the gospel, was at one time in his life perfectly content with a secondhand religion and the external performance of religious duties. Aboard his slave ship on Sunday he faithfully read the prescribed religious service for the day. During the week he read his Bible topside. But while he read his Bible each day and conducted the worship service on Sunday, he could hear the poor, enchained, and miserable slaves groaning in pain under the terrible conditions in the hold of the ship below. After he came under the influence of the Great Awakening evangelists John Wesley and George Whitefield, he exchanged his secondhand religion for a firsthand experience that made a significant difference in his life. Out of this new experience he wrote the most popular Christian hymn today—"Amazing Grace."

Those who accept a creed or a set of propositions of faith, if received as a substitute for an experience by faith, have succumbed to a secondhand religion. Their faith becomes *the* faith in creeds or propositions of faith. Unfortunately, a creed and a set of propositions quickly give the impression that a response to the gospel is primarily one of intellectual assent to certain doctrines rather than a life response to a person. Words can never transmit all that the presence of a person does. Confessions, creeds, and propositions may have served a useful purpose, but it was limited. The great danger comes when these are accepted as definitive for all times and circumstances.

We have considered those who worship God in the shadows of familiarity and a secondhand religion. Now we come to the third shadow, a last resort.

A Last Resort

There are some who think they are sufficient in themselves to cope with the circumstances of life. They take a macho and courageous stand as though they are the "master of their fate and the captain of their souls" and "the menace of the years finds them unafraid." It is not that they do not believe in God, but they use God as a reserve fund on which to turn when resources fail. God is considered a philanthropic magician who is put on a shelf until one comes to the end of the rope. God becomes nothing more than a life preserver to keep one afloat after falling overboard into a sea of trouble, or a spare tire to be used only in case of emergency.

During World War II we became aware of the expression "foxhole" religion. Those men in military service who never had taken time to reflect on God, in the face of enemy attacks and the possibility of being killed, cried out to God in desperation. However, foxhole religion is not the noblest kind. It can be quite superficial, insincere, and short-lived. To be sure, it is better to pray to God in the time of a crisis than not to pray at all. I have known some men in the military service who bragged about God sparing their lives. They liked to acknowledge that God gave them some kind of special protection. Yet there was nothing about their manner of life after the war to indicate that they were truly grateful to God. God got them out of one difficult situation, and they would wait until a similar condition arose to make a mature commitment to Christ.

Admittedly, there were servicemen who continued to rely on God after their foxhole religious experience. They returned from war to take an active part in witnessing to the power of God, though they had not done so before. This sort of experience prompted a large number to enter the ministry. Theological schools became crowded with seminarians. This extraordinary occurrence was welcomed by Roman Catholics, Protestants, and Jews alike.

The Old Testament is replete with examples of unfaithfulness on the part of Israel, but when the backs of the people were pushed against the wall of despair, they cried out to God for help. Their extremity was God's opportunity. Psalm 106 is a classic portrayal of the perversity and obtuseness of the Hebrew people. It gives the history of the use of God as a last resort.

Why do some Christians wait until they are desperate and need help before they realize that their real source of strength is in God? Simply because they worship God as a last resort and do not depend upon a continuing vital relationship with Him.

Chapter 7

Profanity and Restricted Sovereignty of God

P rofanity and restricted sovereignty of God show disrespect for the Almighty. Profanity downgrades the character of God, while restricting God's sovereignty diminishes God's authority and power over all creation.

Profanity

Normally Christians use the words cursing, swearing, blasphemy, and profanity to mean the same thing. Although most dictionaries equate the terms, there is a big difference. We may classify cursing, swearing, and blasphemy as "disrespectable" profanity, whereas "respectable" profanity includes failure to speak in defense of God and godly things, making claims upon God that are uncharacteristic of God, and hiding in pious religiosity.

Disrespectable Profanity

Cursing is the utilization of imprecise language against someone. In many of the psalms the psalmist invoked curses upon the enemies of Israel or upon those who inflicted injuries on persons. A curse was a plea to God to bring evil on those who annoyed the Hebrews. We hear similar expletives today such as "God damn you," "Plague take you," "Go to hell," or "May the devil take you."

According to the Ten Commandments, swearing in the name of God was allowed: "You shall not make wrongful use of the name of the Lord your God" (Exod 20:7). However, a warning was attached. To take God's name in vain was to swear by God's name that what was taken as an oath was true, and if it was not true, the speaker degraded God's name.

In the Sermon on the Mount Jesus said, "You have heard that it was said to those of ancient times, 'You shall not swear falsely, but carry out the vows you have made to the Lord.' But I say to you, Do not swear at all" (Matt 5:33). "You have heard" is not an exact citation from the Old Testament, but rather a conflation or summary of Leviticus 19:12, Exodus 20:7, Numbers 30:2, and Deuteronomy 5:11 and 23:22. All of these verses are directly or indirectly connected with the third commandment. The Jews were allowed to call upon God as a witness to assure others that they would complete their vows and be truthful in the testimony rendered. They were cautioned, however, to be certain that they fulfilled their oaths and told the truth. Otherwise, their vows meant nothing, and their credibility was questioned. In addition—and this was far more sinful—they had no respect for God by whom they swore. Consequently, they dishonored the character of God.

The rabbis tried to dissuade the Jews from taking oaths they could not keep. They taught that an oath was not binding as long as God's name was not included. This teaching gave rise to the Jews taking an oath and circumventing the name of God. They could swear by objects relating to worship such as the Temple, the gold of the Temple, the altar, or heaven. But this led people to believe oaths were not binding.

At the same time the evasion gave the vows a sort of religious coloration as though they were binding.

Contrary to what the third commandment and the teachings of the rabbis in his time allowed, Jesus banned all oaths. By doing this he abrogated the law concerning oaths, and instead of vows he set forth the principle of absolute truthfulness. When persons are honest, all oaths are superfluous. The words of truthful individuals are more trustworthy than the words of liars no matter how much they embellish their testimony with a solemn oath. Those who have a reputation for honesty do not need an oath to decorate their veracity.

Today we might not find in Christian circles those who swear by God to keep a vow or tell the truth, but some do use circumventions that are just as ridiculous as those of the Pharisees. Frequently there are those who will deceive the community into believing they are telling the truth. They use expressions such as "God revealed to me that this is what He wants us to do," "It is the will of God that we embark upon this venture in the church," or "If I do not raise a certain amount of money, God is going to kill me." In some cases ministers appeal to an authority received through ordination as a means of validating their integrity.

Blasphemy is the transliteration of a Greek word that means to speak evil of someone. In the New Testament it means to speak irreverently of God. Profanity is a combination of the Latin preposition *pro* ("before") and the noun *fanum* ("temple"). Thus it means anything not connected with or disrespectful of religious matters. Usually we think of blasphemy, cursing, swearing, and profanity as vulgar, indecent, crude language. Such language comes before us in swearing by God, Holy Jesus, damn, the son of a mother dog, hell, heck, by heaven, darn, and euphemisms for God such as golly, gosh, and for goodness sake. But this crude language does not cover all that is blasphemous or profane. There are other ways of showing contempt for people and irreverence toward God.

Respectable Profanity

Profanity and blasphemy are *any* words, actions, or attitudes that cheapen our view of God revealed in Christ. They are any thoughts that compromise the glory of God with the passing fancy of the temporal. We have what may be called "respectable" profanity or blasphemy. This respectable type can be silent, verbal, or pious.

William Tyndale was the first to translate into English the Erasmus text of the Greek New Testament and parts of the Hebrew text of the Old Testament. Through the instrumentality of Spanish and British ecclesiastics Tyndale was arrested in Antwerp, Belgium, and imprisoned in the Castle of Vilvorde. He was tried and convicted for heresy because he dared to make a translation from the Greek and Hebrew texts rather than from the standardized Latin Vulgate. Just before he was strangled and his body burned, he spoke these words: "Lord, open the king of England's eyes." When Tyndale was condemned, not one word was spoken in his behalf. All the prayers and sermons failed to produce someone to plead for him. This was a profanity of silence.

In the 1930s when Hitler was slaughtering Jews by the millions, where was the voice from the pulpit? Where were those so-called Christians in Germany and other countries when it was essential to protest Hitler's atrocities? Yes, there were a few outcries from pulpits in Germany, the United States, England, and France deploring the genocide, but the majority probably said, "Well it is not happening to us," or they consoled their consciences by writing it off as just being

Jews. Through silent profanity the holocaust was condemned to Christianity.

In 1954 the Supreme Court handed down a decision on equal rights for African Americans. The South took no initiative in upholding this decision, however. It took the civil rights marches and sit-ins led by Martin Luther King, Jr. in the 1960s to promote adherance to the new law. Few religious leaders in the South supported King and others of his race. Before the Supreme Court declared the legality of civil rights, Christians should have been moving rapidly toward this end. Yet their prejudices acquired over the years inhibited them. They became guilty of profanity of silence. Now that equal rights are recognized throughout the United States, some Christian communions have gone on record repenting of the sinful slavery system of their forebears of the last century and have asked for forgiveness. However, nothing has been said about the profanity of silence in the 1960s when civil rights for African Americans was an issue.

Wherever there is corruption in politics, wherever there is inhumanity to others by brutality, wherever the rights of human beings are violated, wherever there is false propaganda and half truths, and whenever some set themselves up as a judge and jury of what is right and what is wrong, Christians are under compulsion to raise a voice of protest. If they do not, they are guilty of the profanity of silence.

Another type of respectable profanity is verbal. Claims are made upon God that make Him less than God. Political parties pray for the success of their candidates. Athletes and coaches pray for victory over their opponents. Prizefighters pray for a decision or a knockout blow in the ring. In the event that all of these are victorious, they are quick to respond that God blessed them. I can hardly think that God takes delight in the verbal bashing and violent blows involved in these contests. Neither is God pleased with persons who verbally condemn those who favor abortion or a homosexual lifestyle.

Also guilty of verbal profanity are those who claim that their prosperity is due to their dedication to God. There are many who boast of their piety and use their wealth as evidence of God's favoritism toward them. They affirm that they are pets of providence. Job in the Old Testament thought that way, too—before calamity hit him. When he lost all his oxen, asses, sheep, camels, servants, sons, and daughters, he could not understand his plight. He did not know of any sin so great to cause this destruction. In addition to these losses, he was afflicted with sores all over his body. His three friends Eliphaz, Bildad, and Zophar were of no comfort to him. They added the traditional views that sin may have brought about his suffering and pled with him to confess his sins.

The author of Psalm 73 was caught up in the same traditional outlook on life. God will help the righteous to prosper, but the unrighteous will lose all—or so he thought. When the psalmist observed what was going on in life, he discovered that this view was not verified by facts. He saw that the wicked were prosperous, their riches increased, and they lived a life of ease and comfort. On the other hand, he perceived that the righteous suffered and were poor. He said that he was envious of the wicked wealthy. It was not until he went into the sanctuary of God that he was able to understand the ultimate futility of the evil, the arrogant, and the proud whose "eyes swell with fatness."

A story is told about a man who constantly bragged about how God had blessed him with prosperity. One day lightning struck his barn and burned everything in it. One of his friends met him after the incident and asked, "Did God bless you when He burned up your barn?" Immediately the man replied, "Taking God up one side and down the other, He does you about as much harm as He does good."

To say as some do that God has blessed them with riches is, indeed, verbal profanity. There are many poor and destitute people who are far more committed to Christ than many of the wealthy. What are we to say to this? Does it mean that God is not the Father of us all as Jesus said in the Lord's prayer? Is God only the God of the prosperous?

A third type of respectable profanity is the pious kind. We can hide in the cloister of respectability but cheapen what is holy. Some use the will of God to clothe their profanity. We have already mentioned the will of God under the shadow of manipulation. While this previous use of the will of God can be profane also, we now look at it in a different dimension.

Some people identify the will of God with tragic circumstances in life. If a loved one is killed by a criminal or on the battlefield or in an accident on the highway, or dies of a fatal disease or drowns, it is difficult for us to understand why, more especially if the victim is young. In our confusion, when the shadows of deepest darkness surround us, there is the temptation to lay the blame on God. Of course, this is done in a pious manner. We may say, "God took him or her," or, "It was the will of God that this should happen." Little do we realize what these statements mean. In a way we are accusing God of murder. Thus, the love of God is frozen into a fatalism devoid of feeling.

Was it the will of God that Jesus should be nailed to a cross? That was one of the opinions in Acts. Blame was laid on Jewish religious leaders and the Romans, but Jesus voluntarily submitted to suffering on the cross to demonstrate the love of God for humanity. The cross shows us how far people will go to get rid of God, but it also demonstrates how much God loves us.

Under the cloak of piety and self-righteousness it is possible for us to relate our personal aims and ambitions to the will of God. We are guilty of profanity when we use the will of God to bolster our own bigotry whether it be in advocating white supremacy, saying our nation is Christian above all other nations, or insisting the political party that yields to the Christian Coalition has the highest morality in our country. In our pride in power, prestige, piety, and progress we must listen again to the poet Francis Thompson who said, "We sweat and brag, then we rot."

We can cheapen and depreciate the character of God by our profanity, but we can also downgrade God by limiting God's control and authority over our lives.

Restricted Sovereignty of God

Every religion that has been fully developed makes a distinction between the holy and the secular. Holiness and sacredness have been restricted to places such as the land of Israel, Mecca and Medina, the river Ganges, the Western Wall in Jerusalem, the church building, the Vatican in Rome, Lourdes in France, or Conyers, Georgia. The holy has been defined as things. Some ministers refer to the pulpit as sacred or holy. The word "holy" has been used in connection with the Bible and the Koran. In addition, rites and rituals such as communion and baptism have been characterized as holy. The word has also prefixed certain persons and words in our religious vocabulary.

Why do we make a distinction between what is holy and what is secular? The whole of creation is sacred and holy. If we believe that God is the God of the universe and is in control, we restrict the sovereignty of God when we draw a boundary line between holy and secular. We can cite numerous examples of this distinction.

The apocalyptists put limits on the power of God when they taught that the world was steeped in evil and immersed in unprecedented pain and suffering, and dominated by tyrannical enemies without and godless leaders within their own ranks. They contended that the world was under the domination of evil forces. The sponsor of wickedness could be a human figure like the Roman emperor or Antiochus Epiphanes or an evil monster called Satan, the devil, Mastema, Beliar, superhuman demons, fallen angels, or demon-possessed persons. Apocalyptists saw the world getting worse and worse, but according to a fixed plan, God would break into history in a cataclysmic manner and destroy the wicked.

The apostle Paul, in writing to the Colossians, declared that there was no value in placating hostile spirits in the planetary regions because Christ had covered every area of life. Again, in his letter to the Ephesians he stated that God had shown the immeasurable greatness of God's power through Christ by the resurrection and had brought into unity all things in heaven and on earth. "God has made him head over all things for the church."

On the surface the reply of Stephen to the accusations made against him by the Sanhedrin seems to be nothing more than a summary of Hebrew history from the time of Abraham to his own time. He began with the God of Majesty who revealed Himself to Abraham in Mesopotamia and commanded him to go to a land he would show him. Abraham received that revelation in a pagan land. Later he referred to the purchase of a burial plot at Shechem. In a crafty manner he made Samaria the center of the patriarchs' inheritance, and thereby shattered the alleged religious superiority of the Jews by implying that the sacred site of Shechem with its nearby shrine had just as much claim to the Hebrew inheritance.

In his build-up of his attack on the Law and the Temple, we tend to pick up from Stephen undertones of an *apologia* for Hellenistic Jews who lived outside the homeland. Stephen was a member of that group of Jews and had probably been reminded time and again that Palestine was the holy land. To those who considered Palestine as the only land that was holy, Stephen seemed to be saying, "it is not true" because God appeared to Abraham in a foreign land.

When Joseph was sold as a slave in Egypt, God delivered him and elevated him to a high position in Pharaoh's court. God was with Moses in the land of Midian, and when Moses was called to deliver the Israelites from Egyptian slavery, he was near Mount Sinai, an area on foreign soil. God commanded Moses to take off his sandals because he was standing on holy ground. God was also with Moses and the Israelites in Egypt before they made their escape, and God continued to go with them in their nomadic existence in the desert.

Clearly and unequivocally, Stephen rejected the Temple and the whole cultic practice. He affirmed that God never intended for the Jews to be shackled by a fixed place for worship, nor did God intend for the rituals to be performed in this institution. Stephen believed that the tabernacle was superior to the Temple. The tabernacle was the pattern from the mount. It was mobile and could be moved from place to place as the Israelites made their way through the desert. The Temple, however, was not constructed until the time of Solomon. Stephen looked upon the construction of this edifice as an act of unfaithfulness to the nomadic character of earlier ideals. He seemed to think that the Jews had made of this religious fixture some sort of idol. They had attempted to confine God to a handbuilt structure. As support for his position he quoted from Isaiah 66:1-2.

Jesus disregarded the taboos of the Pharisees and ate with the outcasts and sinners. It was not only his contact with the sinners that made Jesus unclean, but also the fact that he ate food that was suspected as not having been tithed. Jesus violated the rules of the Pharisees concerning the Sabbath. One of the Ten Commandments said, "Remember the sabbath day to keep it holy." The Pharisees had constructed many regulations as a hedge around this commandment to guarantee that the Jews would keep the Sabbath holy. Some of these rules were unbearable. But you remember that Jesus violated the rules of work and healing on the Sabbath simply because, as he said, "the Sabbath was made for humankind, and not humankind for the sabbath" (Mark 2:27). Should one do good or evil on the Sabbath?

At one time in America we had rules similar to those of the Pharisees, though perhaps not as stringent. Until recent years some states had blue laws restricting what citizens could do on Sunday. They considered Sunday to be a Sabbath day just as the Jews observed Saturday as their Sabbath. Some of these laws date back to strict puritanical regulations prevalent in New England. They encompassed the prohibition of dancing, sports, and buying and selling on Sunday. One of the puritanical rules forbade a man to kiss his wife in public on Sunday after he had returned from a lengthy journey.

The blue laws meant that Sunday was a holy day. But what about the Jews who were citizens of the United States? There were no laws protecting their Sabbath. The millions of Muslims in our country today could demand that Friday become a holy day. The protection of Sunday as a holy day in the past was based on the assumption that the United States was a Christian nation. We know this is far from the truth. There is no day holier than another. All are the creation of God. It so happens that Sunday is the day Christ was raised from the dead, and we use this day to commemorate that event.

The great theme of the Protestant Reformation was the eradication of religious specialization and the release of the devotional life of the monastery to the world. The goal was to permeate every home, workshop, and place of business with the spirit of devotion. Persons could pray to God anywhere, confess God directly, and meditate on a biblical passage as they put a shoe on a horse or made a pair of pants. They took the holy life into the world to transform the world.

Some believers have followed the command, "Come out from among them and be separate," and have withdrawn from the world to preserve their experience of faith in religious gatherings. Yet Jesus said in John 17:15, "I am not asking you to take them out of the world, but I ask you to protect them from the evil one." We are not to be separated from the world; rather, we are to be separated unto God to live the Christlike life in the world.

There are those who take pious delight in referring to the church building as God's house, to the land of Israel as a holy land, or to a prayer room in a church as holy, but these places are no more holy than the place where you live provided you seek God's will. All lands, all places, and all things are holy and sacred because God does not restrict God's sovereignty. The more we try to limit God's sovereignty to this or that place or thing, life becomes less holy, and the demonic takes over. As far as God is concerned, all that exists comes under the rubric of holy. Whatever has been classified as secular or profane has been made such or so designated by Christians.

Those who attempt to limit God's sovereignty with taboos, a series of restraints, or a damper on freedom in Christ say that you cannot do a certain thing or frequent a certain place because evil resides there. This limitation reduces God to the level of the demonic. The more we put limitations on the sacred and the holy, the more we push God out on the fringes of life and allow evil to triumph. If Christianity is just an emptying process, it can hold little concern for us. Our experience in Christ is one that fills. Jesus said, "I came that they may have life, and have it more abundantly" (John 10:10b). May God help us to cease worshiping Him in the shadow of restricted sovereignty.

By respectable and disrespectable profanity, whether it be verbal or silent, God's character comes under attack. If by our inaction or speech we take a stance that is contrary to Christian principles, we lower the character of God before the people to whom we bear witness. If we try to limit God to a place or a thing, God's power and greatness are limited.

Chapter 8

Achievement as the Goal

Villiam Wordsworth was right when he said, "The world is too much with us, late and soon, getting and spending, we lay waste our powers."[1] Indeed, we do "lay waste our powers" in a world dominated by an achievement standard of success. The structure of our day is an achievement culture. To be is to produce, to produce is to achieve, and to achieve is to be a success. It matters little what we produce as long as it is in huge quantities. Quality is not too important, unless the producer makes false claims about his or her goods being superior. In this kind of culture honesty, justice, mercy, and concern for humanity become irrelevant.

Our achievement culture has hit the church broadside with its missiles, and we are in danger of losing the precious cargo of spiritual values. We may glory in society geared for success, mingle in it, work in it, and become prosperous in it, but we are not to be colored by it, nor are we to be fashioned by its image.

In an address to the students of Oxford University in 1941, the late Archbishop Temple said,

> The world, as we live in it, is like a shop window in which some mischievous person has gained access overnight and shifted all the price tags around. The cheap things are priced high, and the really precious things are priced low. My soul, we let ourselves be taken in.

What obtained in 1941, as expressed by the Archbishop, also obtains in the Christian community today. Many of the treasured values of the Christian faith have been cheapened in order to make our witness more appealing to people.

The phrases "a right sense of values," "putting first things first," "getting things in proper focus," "finding a goal in life," "establishing priorities," and "promoting traditional values" are common sayings in business, politics, economics, and religion. All of these phrases are involved in selecting what is important and placing the accent on the proper perspective in achieving the greatest results. However, our environment is for the most part dependent on a character structure denounced by the teachings of Christ.

Jesus taught us not to be overly anxious, but our culture receives its daily nourishment from the creation and cultivation of anxiety. Jesus also said, "Whoever wishes to be great among you must be your servant, and whoever would be first among you must be your servant" (Matt 20:26), but our culture tricks us into the acceptance of greatness through power. We must be big, think big, and stifle the competition. Rewards come to those who succeed. Some receive the honor of being the highest paid athletes in history; CEOs make more money than they will ever use; university coaches' salaries put professors in the category of common laborers; and those in the domain of entertainment skyrocket to success and fortune overnight. If the achievement is not favored with large sums of money, the reward may be fame, awards, trophies, or medals.

In his obelisk that stands in a park in Oslo, Norway, the sculptor Vigoland clearly demonstrates the scramble of people to get to the top. Starting at the bottom of the pyramid, we see the struggle of humanity to reach the apex. The people carved in the pyramid illustrate the highly competitive society in which we live. They are scratching, fighting, biting, kicking, and clawing their way to the upper level.

The worldly standard of success is so dominant that we are tempted to seek rewards of recognition for dedication to Christ. Do you ever ask, "What am I going to get out of it?" For Christians to have this attitude is a clear indication that they are on the track where honesty, integrity, justice, mercy, and love for others become irrelevant. How many people can distinguish between false and true greatness? Perversely enough, it is the spurious type toward which many gravitate. They accept the greatness and success that come from being called great or successful. Genuine greatness is to be found in a person of integrity, compassion, humility, discipline, generosity, and love. In short, true greatness is discovered in those who pattern their lives after the character of Christ.

The effort to be significant involves us in a secret struggle within ourselves and with our contemporaries for a recognized place in society. Everybody wants to be somebody. Nobody is content with being a member of the pack. It is no wonder that Jesus had trouble communicating the purpose of his mission to his disciples. His efforts were frustrated by his hearers' preoccupation with their own selfish interests. If the disciples were not immune from this disease, then neither are we.

On the eve of the crucifixion Jesus in a very dramatic way set an example for his disciples to follow (John 13:1-17). This event is peculiar to John's Gospel. From Luke's Gospel we note that the disciples at the Last Supper were disputing among themselves concerning who would be the greatest (22:24-27). While the rivalry is not mentioned in John's Gospel, we are well aware of it. The jockeying for position explains their sulky and unbecoming behavior in refusing to observe the basic courtesies toward each other. Not one of them was willing to stoop to the menial task of removing the sandals and washing the feet of the others. There they sat, silent and sullen, each proving that he was great as, if not greater than, the others. At that moment Jesus arose, removed his outer robe, poured water into a basin, took a towel, and without saying a word washed the disciples' feet. Imagine the shattering impact of that simple act! The Master of the universe performed the work of a slave while his disciples nourished infantile ideas of greatness. After Jesus finished his task he said to his disciples, "So if I, your Lord and Teacher, have washed your feet, you also ought to wash one another's feet" (13:14).

Jesus sought to change the objects of humanity's quest. He seriously questioned what people set for themselves as goals in life—wealth, power, fame, and sensual pleasures. He reminded us that though we live on earth, we belong to a higher order of existence, and we are to follow principles. He gave us a new order of values, and God's rule topped the list. Before we give in to the popular concept of success, it is incumbent on us to evaluate things properly. This we cannot do until we are in a right relationship with God and submit to God's will.

Jesus taught us a new way of measuring greatness and success. We see this from the very outset in the gospel narrative. He was not born in a palace, or of wealthy parents, or in the capital city of Jerusalem. In his teachings he said, "The first shall be last and the last first. Whoever humbles himself shall be exalted, and whoever exalts himself shall be abased. The greatest among you is to be servant of all. He came not to be served but to serve and give his life as a liberation for many. What does it profit a man to gain the whole world and lose his life?" Thus, Jesus upset the standard of achievement upheld by humanity. He set aside those things to which we cling selfishly and hold on to with dear life. By showing us what God means by greatness, Jesus revolutionized the criterion of success.

Horace Greeley, the famous journalist and political leader known for his slogan, "Go west, young man," said as he neared death: "Fame is vapor, popularity is an accident, riches take wings, those who cheer you today will curse you tomorrow. There is one thing that lasts. It is character."[2] Similarly, in his "Elegy Written in a Country Churchyard" Thomas Gray, while musing over those buried in the churchyard, imagined what some of those ignoble dead might have been. There was some inglorious Milton or perhaps a Cromwell though less guilty of his country's blood. They were "far from the maddening crowd's ignoble strife." However, "their lot forbade to wade through slaughter to the throne," and they did not shut the gates of mercy on mankind. Gray went on to say:

> Let not Ambition mock their useful toil,
> Their homely joys, and destiny obscure;
> Nor Grandeur hear with a disdainful smile,
> The short and simple annals of the poor.
>
> The boast of heraldry, the pomp of power,
> And all that beauty, all that wealth e'er gave,
> Awaits alike th'inevitable hour.
> The paths of glory lead but to the grave.[3]

Our achievement culture has severely damaged the churches in our land. There is a tendency to define greatness and success in terms employed by the business world. We must have the greatest number of members, the largest number in Sunday School, the largest crowds in church services, the biggest budget, and the highest salaries for the church staff. We play the numbers game because we are under compulsion to compete. Some use phrases in relation to the church that are similar to a corporation. They say it is "big business," or they talk about "running a church," "projecting programs," and "submitting a prospectus."

We can get so hypnotized by our church talk, which can result in meaningless chatter, that it is almost impossible to view our commitment objectively. Many outsiders see churches as big business operations, and the truths of Christ are perverted by economic principles of success. They suspect there is more interest in success than in living according to the principles of Christ. They see an emphasis on quantity, not quality. Is it true when unbelievers say that there is not enough difference between those on the inside of the church and those on the outside to make any significant contrast? If this statement is valid, we stand condemned for professing faith and failing to comply with the demands laid on us by Christ.

Christ's death on the cross means that Christians are to live an unusual way of life. By unusual I do not mean odd, for in that case many could be counted as dedicated followers. By unusual I mean a manner of living that is above and beyond the pattern accepted by those who do not claim to be Christian. Jesus said, "What more are you doing than others?" The differentia of Christianity is the surplus, and *in hoc signo vinces* ("in this sign you will conquer"). If our Christian experience does not commit us to something higher in life, it will not be long before we are bored and will yawn at our experience.

Television evangelists and ministers of mega churches quite frequently become performers. Instead of being proclaimers of the good news, they put on a stage performance and entertain the listeners. When I hear them, I am reminded of the Shakespeare play *Hamlet*. When Polonius questioned, "What are you reading?" Hamlet replied, "Words."

Lewis Reamey was custodian of First Baptist Church in Roanoke, Virginia, for many years. He continued to perform his duties in his eighties. He had observed many ministers in that church during his tenure. While I was preaching there, cccasionally I would sit down with Lewis and give him a summary of the sermon I was preparing to preach on Sunday. Looking back on those days, I now see that Lewis was my mentor in ministry. During one of those sessions with Lewis he remarked, "Reverend Smith, we have had preachers to come to this church, and they have painted beautiful flowers on the walls of this church and watered them with their imagination." Then he went on to say, "What if you were invited to a dinner, and you sat at the table expecting to enjoy a delicious meal? Suddenly, the lids on the covered dishes were removed. What did you see? Nothing but sawdust. That is what many people get when they come to hear a sermon."

The congregation will always get sawdust and flowery speeches watered with the imagination if the minister is a huckster of the gospel of Christ. When members of a church diminish in number, the financial obligations of the church cannot be met, and attendance drops off, the temptation is to get a minister who can liven up the congregation and at the same time attract others to attend the church. The church calls a pastor, and s/he comes with a Phineas T. Barnum's bag of tricks to entertain the people rather than depend on the power of God. S/he gives the members what they want rather than what they need. His/Her message is watered down to make it more palatable to the congregation. Rather than give the people the *vox dei* ("the voice of God"), the pastor may reduce his/her message to the *vox populi* ("the voice of the people"). What s/he preaches can become the reflection of the thoughts of the congregation.

There have always been those who are so clever that God cannot use them. They cannot do God's work because they are so fascinated with themselves. They empty their guns on jack rabbits when there are wolves, tigers, and lions in the street.

Those who listen to them are, as someone has said, "in danger of being snowed under with a blanket of conventional religiosity as superficial and shoddy as anything known in history."

Many years ago I attended a denominational meeting in Arkansas. During the course of the meeting a pastor delivered the evangelistic sermon. I do not remember his exact words in one part of his sermon, but this is the impression I got. His remarks were indeed pompous. He thought that God had been piddling around for hundreds of years trying to evangelize the world, but with the appearance of that particular denomination he was assured that God's work was in safe hands. God could just sit down and take it easy. The pastor was so immersed in achievement that he committed blasphemy of the worst sort.

We have enough charlatans, quacks, and pretenders in Christian service who seek to glorify themselves rather than reflect the glory of God in Jesus Christ. To experience the glory of God in the face of Jesus Christ, and to be called to share that knowledge, is the most treasured of all possessions. Such a treasure as this surely must have a container commensurate with it. Certainly there must be a proportionate vessel to safeguard the treasure of inestimable worth. However, to our great surprise, the apostle Paul shatters our pride by telling us this treasure is in earthen vessels (2 Cor 4:7). "The light of the knowledge of the glory of God in the face of Jesus Christ" is found in frail bodies subject to weakness, exhaustion, limitations, infirmities, and decay. It is a treasure in frail minds filled with confusion, weak and warped ideas, prejudice, and jealousy. It is safeguarded in a fragile moral and spiritual nature subject to distortions.

It is so easy for a container to become the center of attention rather than the treasure in the container. In rabbinical literature there is a legend about Rabbi Joshua ben Chananya who was serving as an adviser to the Roman emperor Trajan. One day the emperor's daughter saw the rabbi. Being greatly displeased because her father had such an aged man in his court, she asked the rabbi, "Why does my father choose an adviser like you when he could have young and brilliant men in his court?" The rabbi did not wish to offend the daughter of Trajan, but asked her, "Why does your father keep the royal wine in the jars of earth rather than in vessels of silver?" She immediately informed the rabbi that he was mistaken, but to be certain about her reply she decided to ask her father. Trajan confirmed the statement of the rabbi, but his daughter was so irritated about being wrong that she poured the royal wine into silver bowls. In a few days the wine was sour. Later the rabbi saw the daughter and asked, "Have you noticed that God puts His choicest treasure in earthen pots, so that the vessels may not draw attention from the treasure?"

Not only is this treasure held in earthen vessels so that the container will not detract from the treasure. It is also placed there so we may recognize that the power to share the treasure is not from ourselves but from God. Who is qualified for this career? No person is qualified on his or her own. We are not sufficient of ourselves. Our sufficiency comes from God. God's work depends upon those who are earthen vessels in which another's jewels are kept, lamps of clay in which another's light shines, and living letters known and read by all and written by the indelible ink of God. God will always have His ministry performed by persons who are willing to understand that the exceeding greatness of power is God's.

In Vergil's *Aneid* there is a most interesting account of the sack of Troy. Since the Trojan wall could not be scaled by the Greeks, they resorted to trickery. They constructed a huge wooden horse and placed within the horse some of their best soldiers. A Greek, sent to deceive the Trojans, told them that the wooden horse was a symbol of peace. The Trojans, elated over the withdrawal of the Greek army, began to tear down the wall and pulled the colossal horse into the city. Cassandra, suspecting some evil design, warned the people:

> Cassandra cried and cursed the unhappy hour,
> Foretold our fate, but by the gods decree
> All heard but none believed her prophecy.
> Mad with zeal and blinded by our fate
> We haul along the horse in solemn state.

Today we have torn down walls of the church to drag in achievement—the machine of our destruction. Do we have a Cassandra to warn us against it? If so, what will our response be? With the help of God let us take up arms against this sea of trouble. Let us remove ourselves from this shadow.

Notes

[1]Robert Shafer, *From Beowulf to Thomas Hardy*, vol. 3 (Madison WI: Odyssey Press, 1944) 207.

[2]Source unknown.

[3]Shafer, 913.

Chapter 9

The Sideshow of Trivialities

I have always been fascinated by the story of the little boy who went to the circus for the first time. His mother gave him enough money for his ticket and an additional amount for the traditional circus refreshments of popcorn, cotton candy, peanuts, ice cream, and soda pop. When the boy returned home, his mother asked him how he liked the clowns, the trapeze artists, and the performances of the elephants, ponies, and lions. He replied, "I didn't see any of that." Somewhat surprised at his answer, the mother asked, "What did you see?" In glowing terms her son told her about the bearded lady, the boa constrictor, the fat man, the fire eater, and the midget. His mother was astonished and exclaimed, "Son, you saw the sideshow. You did not get under the main tent."

Equally shocking is the realization that many Christians never get under the main tent in the Christian faith. They are still in the sideshow, giving big loyalties to little insights and fidelity to petty matters on the fringe of religion. They are endlessly preoccupied with the irrelevant and unimportant. Their concern is with externals, not the inner depth of meaning. Through the centuries Christianity has been plagued with new ideas and doctrines that are nothing more than trivialities.

Jesus was deeply disturbed by the emptiness and futility of religious talk that was not translated into character and action. He was opposed to the Jewish leaders because they were meticulous about minor matters, but careless concerning important aspects of religious faith. In the Sermon on the Mount he said, "Unless your righteousness exceeds that of the scribes and Pharisees, you will never enter the kingdom of heaven" (Matt 5:20).

There is no greater enemy to true religion than a showy and pretentious religiosity that has degenerated into triviality or worse. That is why Jesus gave hypocrisy a high priority among the sins he condemned. No one has much use for con artists, quack physicians, or hypocrites in religion. They are always playing a role that never squares with the real character of the person. Hypocrites are not those who fail to live up to their ideals, but those who do not make any effort to do so. There is no attempt to permit behavior to measure up to their profession.

Hypocrisy can move in one of two directions. Persons can pretend to be good, honest, truthful, and sound morally and spiritually when in reality evil is always present. Their goodness is merely a smoke screen to cover up malicious plans to exploit people. Hypocrisy may also take another direction. In this form of hypocrisy vice and evil are not concealed behind a semblance of virtue, but rather the evil is permitted to cover the good because expediency demands it. Someone can be very good in heart and thought, but under the pressure of some kind of fear they are tempted to conform to the voice of the status quo, which can be sinful. Whoever gives in to the pressure puts on a mask of evil and hides the genuine goodness that resides within.

A classic example of the latter form of hypocrisy meets us in the letter of the apostle Paul to the Galatians (2:11-24).

Simon Peter knew that it was right to have table fellowship with the Gentile Christians in Antioch of Syria. When he went to the house of Cornelius in Caesarea, he had understood that God did not make any discrimination between Jew and Gentile (Acts 10:34-38). However, when the alleged delegation from James came to Antioch, Peter, fearing that he might have to answer again to the Jerusalem church for his actions, discontinued his table fellowship with the Gentiles. Paul reprimanded Peter for discrimination and exposed him as a hypocrite.

The former type of hypocrisy comes before us in Matthew 23. Jesus spoke to the crowds and his disciples, warning them about the hypocrisy of the scribes and Pharisees (vv. 1-12), and then directed a series of judgments against them (vv. 13-36). He condemned them for their hypocrisy, self-satisfaction, emphasis on trivialities, and cruelty hidden under a mask of virtue. These were perhaps the most scathing and severe words Jesus ever uttered.

Many Jewish scholars today object to the unfavorable report given about the Pharisees in the New Testament. They question whether the vices castigated by Jesus were typical of the Pharisees as a whole or of merely a small minority of the group. The Babylonian Talmud at the end of the fifth century AD records seven types of Pharisees. In Sotah 22b we find the list:

- "Shoulder" Pharisees wore their good acts on their shoulders for all to admire.
- "Wait-a-bit" Pharisees said, in effect, "Wait-a-bit until I do a good deed that is waiting to be done."
- "Bruised" Pharisees would prefer to run into a wall and bruise themselves rather than look on a woman.

- "Pestle" Pharisees always walked with their heads down in mock humility like a pestle in a mortar.
- "Reckon-it-up" Pharisees always counted their good deeds to see if they were sufficient to counterbalance the evil deeds.
- "God-fearing" Pharisees were like Job.
- "God-loving" Pharisees, like Abraham, were friends of God.

In addition to the self-criticism of the Pharisees by the Babylonian Talmud, they were divided into two schools of thought. Some were followers of Hillel, who introduced a liberal interpretation of the Law. Others became disciples of Shammai, who represented a conservative point of view. Since religious leaders were more legalistic in their interpretation of religion to make a show of their piety and stress the nonessentials, possibly the violent outbursts of Jesus were directed against the followers of Shammai.

While the Gospels give more space to the unfavorable side of the Pharisees than to the favorable, an observant reader can discover sayings and incidents in the life of Jesus that clearly indicate Jesus was not at odds with all of them. Repeatedly he was invited to dine with Pharisees (Luke 7:35; 11:37; 14:1). The Pharisees were the first to warn Jesus about the plot of Herod Antipas against his life (Luke 13:31). Joseph of Arimathea, the man who made arrangements with Pontius Pilate for the burial of Jesus, probably was a Pharisee (Mark 15:43; Luke 23:50). Nicodemus, a Pharisee, went to Jesus to ask some questions (John 3:1).

Yes, there were good Pharisees and bad Pharisees, just as there are good Christians and bad Christians. They were guilty of the same types of hypocrisy as Christians are today. But Jesus condemned the religious leaders for actions other than pretending they were pious, wearing a costume of devotion, claiming social honors, and seeking public recognition. He passed judgment on them for their meticulous attention to minor matters and carelessness concerning important aspects of religious faith. In other words, they were vigilant in the fulfillment of trivialities deduced from their interpretation of the Law. The rabbis of the first century AD attempted to distinguish between what was heavy and what was light in the Law. Perhaps some of them adhered to the principle of Judah, the patriarch of the second century AD who compiled the oral law known as the Mishnah. Judah said, "Be heedful of a light precept as of a weighty one, for you know not the recompense of reward of each precept" (Aboth 2:1).

Jesus noticed that the Pharisees were very careful about determining their tithe. He did not denounce them for tithing. He knew that the Deuteronomic law was binding on them (Deut 14:22). The law required a tithe of grain, wine, oil, and animals, but said nothing about vegetables, nuts, and fruits. The Pharisees added the latter items to the list. According to the Mishnah, the rabbis demanded that dill and cummin be tithed for use as condiments and medicine, but mint was exempt from the tithe. Since the Pharisees represented the middle class of merchants, physicians, and landowners, they could say that the tithe did not apply to their products and income. Thus, some of them wishing to show that they obeyed the Deuteronomic law raised garden vegetables and gave in a scrupulous manner. In their diligence to meet the requirements of the tithe, they overlooked faith, justice, and mercy—which were important in the eyes of God. By spending time on the trivial, they dismissed what was most significant. The three essentials given by Jesus are reminiscent of the classical demands of prophetic religion announced by Micah 6:8.

In a hyperbolical statement Jesus further illustrated the frivolity of the Pharisees. He said that they were very careful to strain out the gnats in preparing the wine, but after all their attentive concern about this impurity, without caution they swallowed a camel. From the Mishnah we learn that the Jews did strain their wine to remove insects. The insects were generated in wine dregs, but they were strained out by means of a cloth or a fine wicker basket. The basis for the filtering was found in Leviticus 11:41, which declared a gnat to be unclean. According to the same scripture, the camel was also unclean. Jesus scathed the religious leaders because they were diligent in straining out the gnats since they were unclean, but they were willing to swallow a much larger unclean thing—a camel. The same inversion of values threatens us. We can fall into the mire and get bogged down with insignificant details while the most important matters of the Christian faith escape our notice.

During the first performance of Gogol's play *Inspector General*, the audience could not refrain from repeated outbursts of laughter at the humorous exposure of the corruption of old Russia. In the midst of the hilarity a voice came from behind the wings of the theater. It was the voice of the dramatist saying, "What are you laughing at? You are laughing at yourselves." We can behold the Jews in Jesus' day and laugh at their calculated religion. The Law told them what was expected, so they thought, and the Pharisees ironed out any uncertainties about what the Law meant. For them, righteousness consisted of doing God's will. Every act of obedience earned merit. The piling up of good works became an end in itself. Thus painstaking devotion to the minutiae of the law was a must. God would pronounce a verdict of righteousness upon those whose good works merited salvation.

Pharisaism boasted in religious devotion, exemplar morality, purity from the world, and almsgiving. Instead of the righteousness of the heart—which expressed the qualities of mercy, sincerity, unselfishness, love, and humility—the Pharisees held to ceremonial and legal righteousness.

While we may laugh at this arid and legalistic kind of religion, we should remind ourselves that our right relationship with God is based on the merciful act of God through Christ. Yet there is always the desire to win God's favor by works' righteousness that really alienates us from God. If this occurs, we shall be laughing at ourselves.

When the Puritans gained control of the British Parliament under Oliver Cromwell in 1653, one of their first resolutions was that no person should be admitted to service in the government until the House of Parliament was satisfied concerning the applicant's genuine godliness. The signs of real godliness in those days were drab clothes, a sour look, a nasal whine, speech interspersed with quaint biblical texts, and an abhorrence of comedies. Among the members of Cromwell's "Little Parliament" of 1653 was a Baptist leather merchant by the name of Praise God Barebone, who more than others was given to strange manifestations of religious piety. His name amused the populace so much that later, in derision of the hypocrisy displayed by him and the Puritan form of government, the 1653 session of Parliament became known as the Barebone's Parliament.

We always live in the dark ages when we specialize in the irrelevant, when we cannot distinguish the essential from the nonessential. To do this is to hold a form of religion but deny that it is a force (2 Tim 3:5). Many of the principles of Christian living that have been transmitted by dedicated people through the centuries are still valid today. Unfortunately, we have received rules that have no relation to Christianity. Even those principles that are valid can be obeyed for the wrong reason. Does obedience come from a master with a whip or through inspiration? Is obedience intended to satisfy the demands of God and gain God's approval, or is it an expression of a peaceful relationship already established? Does obedience seek to satisfy the pressure of public opinion in the community, or is it a response to the overflow of God's love in Christ?

H. G. Wells in his *Outline of History* recounts an interesting story about the adventures of Marco Polo. In 1269 Polo went to the court of the emperor Kubla Khan, the ruler of China, central Asia, and parts of Russia. In conversations with the emperor, Marco Polo told him about Christianity. The emperor was interested and requested that Marco Polo ask the Pope to send him 100 missionaries so that his people could be taught the message of Christ. When Polo returned to Rome, the papacy was vacant. The rival factions in the College of Cardinals could not agree on a new Pope. Finally after ten years Gregory X was named Pope. At the request of Marco Polo, Gregory sent two Dominican friars to convert the greatest power in Asia to Christ. Unfortunately, one of the missionaries died on the journey, and the other one returned to Rome after he reached Armenia. All Asia was a field white unto harvest, but there was no one to reap the harvest. Why the grand stall? Simply because the Church was discussing who should be Pope. While the Roman church did little, the Muslims were making great inroads into China with trade and the spread of Islam.

Too often we get involved in discussions over trivialities and forget our true mission in the world. In modern America the most intense frictions do not arise from interdenominational encounters, but from intradenominational conflicts. Sometimes these factions are doctrinal, but more frequently they are political. The camps are divided into fundamentalists and liberals. When liberals and fundamentalists engage in conversation, pandemonium often results. To confound the other group, each side raises its voice; but the noise only brings sound and fury, thereby signifying nothing.

Liberals and fundamentalists read the Scriptures differently, interpret the traditions differently, and formulate different doctrinal forms. They do not share the same theological language. Liberals condemn fundamentalists for their rigid dogmatism, self-righteous judgmentalism, and simpleminded fundamentalism. Fundamentalists condemn liberals for their tolerance of everything and their spineless posture. Can there be any hope of finding a demilitarized zone? There is no suggestion that each group trades off to such an extent that both are left holding an empty bag. Rather than crucify Christ afresh, surely there can be found a common ground on which we can live and let live. The liberals believe in fundamentals of Christian faith, and the fundamentalists believe in liberality. Unless Christians present a unified front, we have little possibility of appealing to unbelievers.

I know that is not proper to arouse people with the old adage, "Look what others are doing," but it should lead to sober thinking. For example, Islam is the fastest growing religion in the world. In 1900 there were about 200 million Muslims. Today the estimate is about one billion. Islam has increased in membership by 468%, while Christianity has increased by 315%. Interestingly enough, there are about six million Muslims in the United States. Forty countries have a vast majority of Muslims. In Nigeria, one of the strongest Southern Baptist mission fields, Islam has increased faster than Christianity. In 1980, 43% of the Nigerians were Muslims, and 49% were Christians. According to current estimates, the population is 52% Muslim and 47% Christian.

Perhaps part of the appeal of Islam is the ability of Muslims to deal with their diversity. Whether they are Sunnites or Shi'ites, rationalists or sufi mystics, they can all be considered part of the Dar Islam. But Christians in general cannot face diversity without conflict. This puts them in the position of worshiping God in the shadow of trivialities.

The many trite, picayunish, piddling, and worthless thoughts and actions that are paraded before the world by some Christians are too numerous for me to mention here. They are found in all communions, in individual churches, and in individuals.

In the fifth act of Henrik Ibsen's play *Peer Gynt,* we see Peer creeping among the undergrowth gathering wild onions. He holds an onion in his hand and decides to let each layer represent some experience in his life. As he names each highlight in his career, he peels off a layer of the onion. From the shipwrecked man to the gold digger in San Fransico, from the pelt hunter by Hudson's Bay to the Muslims' prophet, Peer casts aside the layers in increasing excitement. Finally, all of the pieces of the onion are gone, and he discovers there is no kernel. There is nothing left of his life but swathings. His life was just a series of incidents without a center. He had not lived for a goal, and there was nothing to hold his life together.

If our lives are overlaid with trivialities in our Christian commitment, one day we shall discover that the love of Christ, the kernel of life, is no longer there.

Trifles and trivialities are nothing more than sideshow attractions. If stripped from our lives, the swathings of propositions of faith, creeds, puritanical piety, loyalty to a political party first and foremost, denominational arrogance, and irrelevant activity in the church could reveal an emptiness of which we are completely unaware.

Chapter 10

Bridging the Gap with Angels

I n preexilic days in the history of Israel, the Hebrew people believed that God was elevated and exalted above them, but remained in touch with humanity. They maintained that God cut a covenant with the patriarchs, gave the Law to Moses at Mount Sinai, led the army of Israel during the conquest of Canaan, sent messages through the prophets to castigate the sinners, and promised deliverance to the righteous. After the exile God became more transcendent. The prophet of the Restoration declared, "For as the heavens are higher than the earth, so are my ways higher than your ways and my thoughts than your thoughts" (Isa 55:9). With this emphasis on the transcendence of God, the Jews were faced with a dilemma. If God is far removed from us, how do we bridge the gap between ourselves and God? The more the theological spirit of the age elevated God to the heavens, the less the Jews believed that God was in touch with humanity.

One solution to the dilemma for Judaism was the introduction of intermediaries between God and God's people. This was accomplished through the speculations of the apocalyptists who developed a hierarchy of angels and thousands of subordinate angels. In Israel's preexilic history the angels were nothing more than manifestations of the majesty of God, but then they became channels by which God communicated to

God's people. In the Greek world before the Hellenistic age, angels were eminently respectable. The Greeks had their *aggeloi* such as Nemesis and Hermes. Plato had spoken about "middle creatures" who moved up and down on earth and through the whole heaven with lightly rushing motions. In the Hellenistic age the Stoics held that god ("reason" or "fire") existed in the world mind and related to the world through an infinite number of seminal powers called the *logoi spermatikoi* ("reason").

There is no basis for the suggestion that this new emphasis on angelic activity in the religion of Israel issued from Hellenistic influence. The Jerusalem Talmud states that the names of angels were brought by the Jews from Babylonia (*Rosh hash Shanah* I.2). The Talmudic witness does not mean that the angels were of Babylonian origin, but of Persian influence while Babylonia was under the dominion of the Persian empire. After the Babylonians were conquered by Cyrus and the Persians and before the Jewish exiles returned to their homeland, there was sufficient time for the Jews to become acquainted with Zoroastrianism, the Persian religion. In the Zoroastrian system Ahura Mazda, the god of light, had ministers, the Amesha Spentas, who carried out his commands.

The Jewish apocalyptic literature that came into existence around 200 BC and continued until about 100 AD introduced a hierarchy of angels. Seven archangels were named: Uriel, Raphael, Gabriel, Raguel, Michael, Remiel, and Saraquel. Each archangel was given a specific assignment. Two are mentioned in the Old Testament and two in the New Testament. In both instances they are Gabriel and Michael. In the book of Daniel, Gabriel is designated as the messenger angel, and Michael is assigned to protect Israel.

According to Luke's Gospel, the angel Gabriel delivered the message to Mary that she was to bear a child, and in the epistle of Jude there is a reference to the apocalyptic writing *The Assumption of Moses* relating the struggle between Michael and the devil over the body of Moses. Michael appears again in Revelation as the warrior angel who defeated Satan and expelled him and his cohorts from heaven. The angels ministered to the people in various ways. They were guardians of individuals and the nation Israel, intercessors in behalf of the Jews before God, communicators of God's message to individuals, and participants in the great eschatological drama.

In the first century AD the Sadducees and the Pharisees differed in their views of angelology. It is commonly believed that the Sadducees erased the notion of angels from their theology. However, they held to the Torah, the first five books of the Old Testament, as their Scriptures. Therefore, they knew that the manifestation of angels appeared in this section of the Bible. Rather it appears that the Sadducees sought to limit the angelic population explosion. They thought that it was inappropriate to personify the divine messengers and to ascribe to them personal names and distinct personalities. In their opinion God alone ruled Israel and was unaided by Gabriel and all the others.

The Pharisees, before the destruction of Jerusalem in AD 70, followed the theological concepts of the apocalyptists and believed in the existence of angels. After the fall of Jerusalem the Pharisees discarded the apocalyptic teachings on angels. They retained the concept of the resurrection from the dead, which was high on the scale of beliefs fostered by these visionaries. From that time on, the rabbis settled down to a concentration on the study of the Torah. The Essenes, another sect of Judaism in the first century AD, adhered to the teaching of angels. This sect possessed communistic and ascetic tendencies and followed the theology of the apocalyptists. The Essenes came to an end after AD 70.

In the Apocrypha there are three references to angels. One is found in the book of Tobit, where Raphael becomes the guardian angel of Tobias, the son of Tobit. In his poverty and blindness Tobit remembered that he had left a large sum of money with a certain Gabael in Rages in Media. Tobias decided to go to Media and get the money. He was accompanied by Raphael who had disguised himself as Azarias, a kinsman of the family. After Tobias and Raphael returned safely from their mission, Raphael revealed himself as one of the seven holy angels who presented the prayers of the saints before the presence of God. On the basis of this apocryphal story, some still believe in guardian angels.

In Bel and the Dragon, apocryphal additions to the book of Daniel, the angel of the Lord lifted Habakkuk by his hair and carried him to Babylon where Daniel had been thrown into a den of lions. Habakkuk took his lunch with him and shared his food with Daniel. The third reference comes from 2 Maccabees. It is a story about Heliodorus, the general of Seleucus IV, the Syrian king. He entered the Temple in Jerusalem to rob the treasury. He did not succeed in his plan, however, because a rider on a horse appeared and beat Heliodorus to such an extent that he had to be carried away on a stretcher. The writer of this document apparently believed the rider was an angel sent by God.

According to Moses Maimonides, the Jewish philosopher of the Middle Ages, the term "angels" applied to human beings, animals, and prophetic ideals. In the *Guide for the Perplexed* he said,

> Angel means messenger; hence every one that is entrusted with a certain mission is an angel ... There is no doubt that the word angel is used of a messenger sent by man (Gen 32:4) or a prophet (Jud 2:1; Num 20:16); it is also used of

ideals perceived by prophets in prophetic visions ... Every appearance of an angel is a part of a prophetic vision, depending on the capacity of the person that perceives it (2:6).

Some of the early Christians allowed their enthusiasm to get the best of them, and they began to worship angels. There seems to be no doubt that a cult of angel worshipers infected the church in Colossae. The apostle Paul wrote a letter to the church in Colossae and chided the congregation for excessive ritualism, asceticism, and worship of angels (2:16-23). The members of the church had been taken in by a Jewish syncretism of astral religion, Greek philosophy, and what was later known as Gnosticism. Paul had never been to the church in Colossae. The Lycus Valley had been evangelized by Epaphras, a fellow worker of the Apostle. When Paul heard of the disquieting news of the activity of false teachers who were trying to lead the Colossians astray, he wrote a letter to the church to correct the erroneous speculations to which they were subjected.

The Apostle did not mince words about his objection to the heresy, but wrote frankly concerning the danger of worshiping the shadows rather than the substance or the real. One of the shadows to which he referred was the worship of angels. Along with angel worship he included festivals, new moon observances, and the Sabbath. These were annual, monthly, and weekly rites. Paul made a reference to food and drink connected with the heresy. This either involved Jewish dietary laws or alluded to Gnostic teachings about matter being evil.

There seems to be no doubt that worship of angels in the church was related to a cult of angels, and it appears that this was the main feature of the heresy. Those who adhered to the cult of angels believed that God was utterly beyond their knowledge, and it was essential that they worship through intermediaries in whom God's knowledge was partially reflected. Members of the church took their stand on visions connected with angel worship, and by this means thought that they possessed a higher illumination. Thus their faith became inflated with sensuous notions. The wisdom that they prided themselves as having by this sort of worship was nothing more than empty imagination. To strengthen his argument, Paul said that Christ covered every area of life. All existence was related to Christ, just as the head was to the body. Christ is the head, and the church is the body of Christ, and through Christ the body (church) grows with the increase of our commitment to God.

Currently in America there seems to be a desire to return to dependence on angels. While few persons would admit that their need for a communication from God through angels results in worship of them, the temptation is always there to do just that. Why do people need angels? Perhaps it is because our age is similar to the Hellenistic period. It is a time of change and upheaval. The changes have brought about a feeling of insecurity. Some people are not able to adjust to the new order of things with the passing of old systems, traditions and loyalties. Perhaps some look upon God as an emeritus God, as One who has become so transcendent that angels are necessary to bridge the gap.

"Touched by an Angel" is a popular TV program today. I watch it every time it shows. For fiction it is an excellent show, but it should not be taken as factual. The writer should be highly commended for the show's inclusiveness and theology. The angels are sent as messengers from God to give support to persons who have problems, yet they are limited in their knowledge and can only surmise what God's intention holds.

The English word for angel is a transliteration of the Greek word *aggelos*, which means "messenger." The Hebrew word *malech* has the same meaning. The messenger may be a human being or a supernatural being. Rather than conjuring up an apparition of the supernatural variety, why not settle for a dedicated Christian who can bring a message from God—like the messengers in "Touched by an Angel." After all, the fullness of God's revelation has been given to us in Christ, and there is no further need for intermediaries to communicate with us. Christ dwells with us, and by that union we are in touch with God.

In addition to those who claim that angels guard their lives or communicate messages to them, there are other visions people have had. In the *Greenville News* on October 4, 1998, there appeared a feature article about a pastor in Charlotte, North Carolina, who saw an image of Christ similar to the impression on the Shroud of Turin. The pastor believed it was a warning of a coming apocalypse and urged the people to repent of their sins before it was too late. Some believers say they have seen images of Christ in the clouds, on a California mountain, on the side of an Ohio oil company storage tank, and even on a burnt tortilla. Multitudes have gathered at Conyers, Georgia, to witness the yearly appearance of the Virgin Mary.

In the days of a new millenium we shall likely hear more reports of visions, angelic messages, and image sightings. Hopefully, people will not be taken in by this kind of revelation. They should bear in mind what Jesus told his disciples in the farewell discourse in the fourth Gospel: that he would not leave them orphans, but would come to them in the form of the Holy Spirit. Christ comes to us today individually and to the community of believers by his Spirit. We are in Christ, and Christ is in us. Therefore, we have no need for intermediaries to bridge the gap between us and God, for this has been accomplished through the revelation of God in Jesus Christ.

Epilogue

A poem that aroused my interest and has had a marked effect on my mind ever since my high school days is the "Lady of Shalott" by Alfred Lord Tennyson. The rhythmical composition tells us of a woman who inhabited a castle on an island in the middle of the river that flowed to Camelot. She was aware that a curse was upon her, but did not know its contents. She was doomed to look at life through a mirror,

> Moving through a mirror clear
> That hangs before her all the year,
> Shadows of the world appear,
> There she sees the highway near
> Winding down to Camelot.

The Lady of Shalott had a loom before her and wove the sights reflected in the mirror. She saw the reapers early in the morning working in the barley fields, lovers returning from saying their marriage vows, and knights riding to and from Camelot. But when she saw Sir Lancelot in all of his splendor, that was her breaking point. She exclaimed, "I am half sick of shadows." The Lady of Shalott dared look at real life, and the mirror cracked. She knew that the curse was upon her. She ran to the willow trees on the bank of the river. There she found a boat, and on the bow of the boat she wrote "The Lady of Shalott." Getting into the boat, she let the current of the river carry her to Camelot. Before reaching her destination, she died.

The Lady of Shalott was cursed with looking at life through shadows. We do not have such a curse except as we are willing to hex ourselves with it. Let us smash the mirror that reflects distortions of God and come to the light of the knowledge of God in the face of Jesus Christ.

If we worship God through shadows rather than in spirit and in truth, this does not make God less. God is not dependent upon us to submit to His sovereignty in order to be God. At times in Israel there was the notion that God had to uphold His honor by rescuing the nation, or else God's name was blasphemed among the pagans. The prophet Ezekiel appealed to God to aid Israel. But God is not diminished in holiness if we fail to respond to God properly. However, we cannot but believe that God is pleased when we recognize His worth and worship removed from the shadows of our own making.

Suppose a person lived among us like Joshua in Joseph Girzone's novel of the same name. Most of the people thought that Joshua was strange in his behavior because he helped people. The theologians could not understand why or how an uneducated man like Joshua could call into question some of the dogmas of the church. They thought he lived in a dream world and was not in touch with reality. He refused to worship God in the shadows of humanity's own concoctions. Customs, practices, and traditions often become barriers to our growth in the love of God and humanity. As adults we continue to cherish the religious practices to which we are accustomed. If there is any change in the customs and traditions, we tend to panic because we have been led to believe that these shadows are part of our faith.

The prophets of the Old Testament, and to a greater degree Jesus, were brave enough to look beyond the limitations of human religious traditions and lead the people to truth. They had the boldness to revoke sterile and rigid religious forms in spite of the fact that they incurred the anger of religious leaders who hated them and wanted to kill them. The religious leaders perceived that Jesus was upsetting the apple cart, and they thought that by having him put to death they were doing God a favor. The shame of religious leaders is the attempt to control religion and people's practice of religion. These leaders are unwilling for people to think for themselves because they may lose control over them. Religious leaders should set an example and persuade others by their own deep faith and by the commitment of their lives. Of course, it is incumbent on religious leaders to teach the believers so that they will have the tools to think for themselves.

Our faith comes alive when we show our love for God and others. When our religion becomes dissociated from everyday matters concerning our living with others, it becomes unreal and powerless. When we lose our grip on God, we lose our grip on ourselves.